EDWARD
HAYS

PRAYERS
for the
DOMESTIC
CHURCH

A handbook for worship in the home

Forest of Peace   Notre Dame, IN

BOOKS BY EDWARD HAYS

PRAYERS AND RITUALS

Psalms for Zero Gravity: Prayers for Life's Emigrants

Prayers for a Planetary Pilgrim: A Personal Manual for
Prayer and Ritual

Prayers for the Domestic Church: A Handbook for Worship
in the Home

Prayers for the Servants of God

PARABLES AND STORIES

The Christmas Eve Storyteller

The Ethiopian Tattoo Shop

The Gospel of Gabriel: The Life of Jesus the Christ

Little Orphan Angela

The Magic Lantern

The Quest for the Flaming Pearl: Tales of St. George and the
Dragon

St. George and the Dragon and the Quest for the Holy Grail

Sundancer: A Mystical Fantasy

Twelve and One-Half Keys

CONTEMPORARY SPIRITUALITY

The Ascent of the Mountain of God

Chasing Joy: Musings on Life in a Bittersweet World

Embrace the Healing Cross: Daily Prayscriptions for Lent

Feathers on the Wind: Reflections for the Lighthearted Soul

The Pilgrimage Way of the Cross

The Great Escape Manual: A Spirituality of Liberation

The Hobo Honeymoon of Lent

Founded in 1865, Ave Maria Press is a ministry of the United States Province of Holy Cross.

www.forestofpeace.com

ISBN-10 0-939516-79-9   ISBN-13 978-0-939516-79-7

Cover and text design by Katherine Robinson Coleman.

Printed and bound in the United States of America.

Library of Congress Cataloging-in-Publication Data

Hays, Edward M.
    Prayers for the domestic church : a handbook for worship in the home / Edward Hays.
        p. cm.
    Originally published: Easton, Kan. : Forest of Peace Books, 1979.
        Includes index.
        ISBN-13: 978-0-939516-79-7 (pbk.)
        ISBN-10: 0-939516-79-9 (pbk.)
        1. Family—Prayers and devotions—English. I. Title.
    BX2170.F3H39 2007
    249—dc22

                                    2007010740

DEDICATED

---

to all those who have come to Shantivanam,

the Forest of Peace, and who, by their prayers,

have made it a house of prayer

and to Archbishop Ignatius J. Strecker

whose vision of a house of prayer

and whose support of Shantivanam

have made it a living reality.

CONTENTS

This handbook of prayers,
  like a mystic river
  rising in the high mountain peaks
  of the great holy books,
  makes its way downward,
  fed into by
  scores of silent streams and hidden springs.
  Winding its way
  among the foothills of tradition and time,
  it flows onward
  til it cascades down the cliffs of change
  into the rich and fertile valley
  of today.

This river of prayer has been
  nourished by numerous people,
  channeled forward
  by the encouragement and kindness of friends.
  The path of this river
  follows the finger of God,
  the Divine Spirit,
  who has led it into your home.

As you now use this handbook of prayer,
  this river will continue to flow on,
  taking in the many arteries
  of your personal and communal life.
  Your prayers will swell its mighty force
  as it surges wide and deep,
  expanding outward into the whole cosmos,
  giving glory to God
  and bringing peace to our earth.

PREFACE
TO THE
NEW
EDITION

I t is an honor to have the opportunity to write a preface for this new edition of my book of prayers and blessings for the Home Church. The prayers in this book were born out of the theology of the Second Vatican Council that reintroduced the apostolic concept of the home as a domestic church. When *Prayers for the Domestic Church* was first published in 1979, it was a pioneering publication. To my knowledge, it was the only handbook available for the non-ordained containing home rituals and blessings that had previously been reserved for the clergy.

Prayers for the Domestic Church is even more valuable today as a resource for any variety of family than when it was first released. The concluding decades of the twentieth century and the beginning ones of the twenty-first have witnessed a major decrease in weekly church attendance by the faithful. This sociological and religious change has created a vacuum that cries out for the home to become a place for worship and prayer just as it was in ancient apostolic centuries.

Regardless of your personal practice of weekly church worship, this book of home blessings and prayers remains an essential tool for spiritual growth. In former ages, ritual blessings were based on a theology that saw their purpose as transforming the various profane objects and places of life and making them holy. Today God, the Holy One, is acknowledged as an abiding reality in the midst of daily life. Therefore, the purpose of blessings—whether of objects, places, or special family times—is not to change them but to awaken us to the already abiding Presence of God within them.

Recent decades have given us a greater and more appropriate appreciation of the majestically powerful gifts of our baptism. By their baptismal anointing, parents and adults are made a priestly people who have God's commission and grace to perform blessings in their homes and to make them dynamic home churches.

Today there are many styles of households. So whatever style of home yours may be, may you grow spiritually in it and become more closely united to those you love by the blessings and prayers within this book.

INTRODUCTION

What is a home? Today's home is founded in unusual as well as traditional patterns. It can be a large, two-story house or a single room. The home can be an apartment where one person lives with another, or a bed in a double room of a retirement home. A home can be a convent or a rectory. It can be a place where one person lives or where a number of persons live as a family. This can be a family of father, mother and children or a family of a single parent and children. (The prayer on pages 48–49 acknowledges this sort of single parent home, which may be created by complex work arrangements or by separation.) Each one of these homes can and should become a domestic church—the place where father, mother and children, or single parent with children, or unmarried person with friends, or groups of religious come together to celebrate their unique relationships with each other and with God.

Many of the prayers in this handbook have been written for the traditional home with ritual roles for the mother and father of the home. These and other aspects may easily be adjusted to fit your life, helping to transform your "home" into a domestic church.

The Domestic and Primal Church: The Home

The first altar around which primitive people worshipped was the hearth, whose open-fire burned in the center of the home. The next altar-shrine was the family table where meals were celebrated and great events in the personal history of the family were remembered. The priests and the priestesses of these first rituals were the fathers and mothers of families. The grandfather (or great-grandfather) of a clan was the chief priest and held the power of blessing. Only later in history were there special persons in society whose expressed duty it was to perform the rituals and blessings of daily life. Even with the rise of an institutional priesthood and of temples outside the home, the home was held sacred and remained the primal place of prayer and worship. Each home had a shrine, its special sacred spot, where family members gathered in times of trouble and in times of rejoicing and remembering, there to bless their God with song and praise.

Early Christianity confirmed this sense of the sacred that encircled the home. For centuries, it was in this most basic of all social structures—the home—that Christians gathered to celebrate the holy meal of the remembrance of the death and resurrection of Jesus. Again, with the passage of time, the home—along with its family-celebrants and its yearly cycle of feasts, festivals, and unique family celebrations—became eclipsed by the emergence of a great church building or cathedral. The communal church of which numerous families were a part was intended to be a gathering point, a collection of churches, we might say—and not a substitute for the domestic church, the home. Families came to the village church bringing the gifts of their domestic liturgies—their family prayers—and these were joined to prayers of other families to form the rich and inspiring prayer-mosaic of the Christian community.

Now, in these first years of the twenty-first century, our attention is again drawn to this basic religious center, this primal domestic church that is the home. Once again, we look upon the home as a place of prayer and worship. We bring forth from the treasury of tradition the customs, rituals, blessings and prayers that find their real beauty when celebrated in the home and by the persons whose lives are directly and intimately touched by them.

We recall again the basic truth of God's revelation, that the first holy ministers of the sacred are the father and mother of each family. Were this ancient and honored position held by all parents to once again be regarded as sacred and revered, we would not need fear a shortage of ministerial persons to service the larger family at the communal church. But for this to happen we need more than a dream, more than a simple wish that our homes become domestic churches; we need to actually begin to make them places of prayer and celebration.

As a first step, each family must select its shrine-place, the holy gathering place for the family at times of prayer. This can be the table, or a corner of a room or simply a spot beneath a religious icon or image. No home is too small or too poor to become a domestic church. How simple are the needs: a candle, a small rug to be used as a prayer mat, a cross, an honored place where the Holy Bible is kept, a statue. . . .

Next, a sense of awareness is necessary that makes special—that makes sacred—the common events of our daily lives. Occasions like birthdays, the purchase of a new car, the need for safety in the face of a storm, a child's first day at school, the anniversary of the death of a parent—these and countless other common events become sources of the domestic liturgy where father and mother become the prime celebrants, and other family members the concelebrants.

Each family is a tiny nation; and, like nations, each family, each household, should have its own set of folk customs and traditions. Special foods and special activities on certain feast days combine to form a living personal family tradition. Any home that does not gift its children with a personal family tradition robs them of a birthright. These domestic traditions need to be simple but real, joyful and not superficially pious, prayerful and playful, so that they will nourish all the members of the family. Such traditions become heirlooms to be passed on from generation to generation as they are illuminated from the inside with beautiful memories and faith.

Perhaps the greatest hurdle in making the home a center of prayer will be overcoming our embarrassment at performing these religious functions. At first we will be ill-at-ease, but the memory of this ancient prayer-custom is rooted in our inner-selves, perhaps etched forever into our DNA code. We have only to rekindle its memory to begin to treasure with reverence the power of blessing that has been asleep for so many years and that belongs to every parent— to every person.

Awakening once again the priestly power of parents and the sacredness of the home will in no way be the cause of a lessening of reverence for the communal or local Church. Rather, we will find our communal churches once again flourishing and flowering with holiness when the gift processions at the offertory of parish Masses include the prayers and worship of each of the domestic churches whose members have come together to celebrate a communal and global celebration of gratitude. For all true worship, whether by a single family or a large parish, is never merely a worship-whirlpool pulling its members inward into themselves; rather, true worship of God fashions a glorious pinwheel of grace and peace whirling outward, touching all, to the limits of the universe and beyond.

BLESSING PRAYERS:
MEETING THE SACRED
IN OUR LIVES

The blessing of persons or objects is not done for the purpose of making them holy, since all that God has created is good and is holy. Rather, blessings call forth a special grace from God to use an object as its artistic creator intended. The blessing of a person is meant to make that person the receiver of light, love and special affection from God and to awaken the person to experience how God uses the ordinary events of life to touch us with divine love.

Blessings are prayers, and as such we can bless things or people as often as we like, as often as these blessings help us see with eyes of faith. The blessing of a home or of a frequently used object, for example, could well occur once a year. In this way, the blessing would act as an annual dedication of the object, as well as a yearly reminder of how our homes are the primal places where we shall create the Kingdom.

Since the grace of the blessing is invisible—real, but not visible—the use of some gesture or instrument can aid us in understanding the mystery of what is taking place. The sign of the cross can be made over a person or object, or it can even be traced on a person's forehead or upon the article being blessed. At times we might also wish to use a crucifix to bless persons or objects. In doing this, the cross is held in the right hand, raised up in the air and then traced over the object or person in the sign of the cross. At special seasons, the sign of the cross is, by custom, traced with a marker upon a wall or door as an outward sign that God's mark has been placed upon the blessed object. Ancient tradition also includes the placing of sacred symbols such as a cross or a medal on that which has been blessed. Holy water is often sprinkled on that which is being blessed. All water is holy, and so, even unblessed water may be used as an outward sign of Life. The use of water that has been specially blessed by the Church carries the extra dimension of a beautiful and grace-full connection between ourselves and the rest of the Church. The imposition of hands upon the head, an embrace or a kiss are other ways of blessing persons and, in certain cases, objects. What is essential in any action or gesture is that it be done slowly and with great reverence as well as with great faith.

The frequent and devout blessing of the people and objects of our day-to-day life will lead us to meet the Divine at every turn. Our prayer will seek the sacred in all the events that confront us, in all the states of life in which we find ourselves. The blessings and prayers in this section of the handbook are intended to encourage this meeting of God's grace at every moment.

We never pray or worship alone; always, we are all part of all that is. All members of the family, and guests as well, should be encouraged to assist in the externalizing of a common blessing. In all our prayers, blessings and dedications, we should strive to become conscious that we pray in union with all the people of God, for what we lack in faith or in commitment is supplied by that greater and global community that we call Church.

This blessing may take place upon moving into a new home, sharpening the family's vision of it as the domestic church. It may also be used as a means of celebrating family tradition and history on the yearly anniversary of moving to the home, or once a year on a great feast such as Christmas or Easter.

An unlit candle may be placed in each room to be blessed, with the additional option of holy water available for sprinkling each room. To begin, the family gathers, weather permitting, outside the front door of the home.

FATHER: Lord our God,
 You whose home is in heaven, on earth . . .
 and in that undiscovered beyond,
 come and bless this house
 which is now to be our home.
Surround this shelter with Your Holy Spirit.
Encompass all its four sides
 with the power of Your protection
 so that no evil or harm will come near.
May that divine blessing
 shield this home from destruction, storm, sickness
 and all that might bring evil
 to us who shall live within these walls.

After a moment of silence, the sign of the cross may be traced—or holy water sprinkled—on the outside of the house or upon the outside of the front door.

Blessed be this doorway.
May all who come to it
be treated with respect and kindness.
May all our comings and goings
be under the seal of God's loving care.

Blessed be all the rooms of this home.
May each of them be holy
and filled with the spirit of happiness.
May no dark powers
ever be given shelter within any of these rooms
but banished as soon as recognized.

18

Mother now leads all gathered to the living room. A can-dle may be lit here and in each following room to be blessed so that at the end the entire house would be illuminated. Or, again, holy water may be used in each room.

MOTHER: Blessed be this living room.
May we truly live within it as people of peace.
May prayer and playfulness
never be strangers within its walls.

all proceed to the dining room

Blessed be this place where we shall eat.
May all our meals
be sacraments of the presence of God
as we are nourished at this altar-table.

all proceed to kitchen

Blessed be this shrine of the kitchen.
Blessed be the herbs and spices,
and the pots and pans used to prepare our meals.
May the ill-seasonings of anger and bitterness
never poison the meals prepared here.

all proceed to bathroom

Blessed be this bathroom.
May the spirits of health and healing abide here
   and teach us to honor and love our bodies.

all proceed to bedroom

Blessed be these bedrooms.
Here we shall find rest, refreshment and renewal.

May the spirits of love and affection,
   together with the spirits of angelic care
   touch all who shall use these rooms.

*all return to the living room where the following conclud-
ing prayer is said:*

Let us pause now and pray in silence
   as each of us calls down the holy blessing of God
   upon this
   house, now become our home.

pause for silent prayer

FATHER: Let us pray as our Lord taught us to pray:
   "Our Father, . . . "

all recite the Lord's Prayer

Lord our God,
   may Your divine name be always holy within our
   home.
May You, as Holy Father and Divine Mother,
   lovingly care for all who shall live here.

May Your kingdom come in this home
   as we love and respect one another.
May we always do Your holy will
   by living in harmony and unity.
May we never suffer from lack of bread,
   from a lack of all that we need
   to nourish our family.

May the spirit of pardon and forgiveness reside with us
     and be always ready to heal our divisions.
May the spirits of mirth and laughter, hope and faith,
     playfulness and prayer, compassion and love
     be perpetual guests in our home.

Mother goes to the door of the home, opens it and prays:

MOTHER: May our door be always open to those in
     need.
Open be this door
     to the neighbor or to the stranger.
May our friends
     who come to us in times of trouble and sorrow,
     find our door open to
     them and to their needs.
May the holy light of God's presence
     shine forth brightly in this home
     and be a blessing for all who shall live here
     and for everyone who shall come to this door.

May God's holy blessing rest upon us all,
     in the name of the Father,
     and of the Son
     and of the Holy Spirit.

Amen†

*The blessing of the home may be followed by a festive meal
where family and guests present would christen the home
with laughter and song.*

Blessing Prayers for Persons Who Live in a Single Room

This blessing may follow a period of personal prayer or meditation.

Lord, this room is to be my home;
    may Your holy power furnish it in peace
    and decorate its four walls with holiness
    so that Your Sacred Presence
    will also abide here.

Lord, it is not large or grand,
    but it is to be my living place.
May I find within its close quarters
    refreshment and Your sacred space.

May the spirit of prayer
    be my frequent guest and welcome roommate.
May the spirit of praise
    guide every task or deed performed here.

Lord, You who love the small and the simple
    and who have designed Your kingdom in that pattern,
    let me find You and the joy of Your kingdom
    in this, my simple room.

For me, Lord, this room will be
    a place for living, sleeping, praying;
    it will be a shrine, a bedroom and a place of
    healing.

May my door stand open to all who are in need
    as a sign of the posture of my heart.

May peace, love and beauty flow out
    from this room of mine
    in all four directions
    and up and down as well.
May Your silent echo be heard
    by all whose lives surround me.

The birds of the air have their nests,
    the foxes their dens;
    may this room of mine
    be blessed by You, my God,
    as a home for me . . .
    and for You as well.

Amen†

A sign of the cross may be traced on the four walls and on the door of the room and a candle lit.

BLESSING PRAYERS
FOR A NEW POSSESSION

Lord God, Creator of All That Is,
    we rejoice in this new possession of ours:_____
We are grateful for the greater quality of life
    that it helps us to enjoy,
    grateful that we have been given the honor
    of being its stewards.
Help us to use this gift
    as You, its Ultimate Source,
    intended it to be used.
May this our possession
    be cause for a healthy pride of ownership
    and give us a willingness to embrace
    all the duties that ownership implies.

Most of all, may we see this_____
    as a sign of Your divine affection
    and continuous care for us.
May we never take for granted
    the numerous good things You have allowed us to share.
As we rejoice in this gift,
    may we remember all of the other things
    that You have done for us in the past.
Let us pause now
    in a prayer of silent gratitude.

    pause for silent reflection

Lord our God, Holy Source of All Grace,
    may Your divine blessing rest upon this_____
    and upon each of us who, today, rejoices in it.

Amen†

BLESSING PRAYER
FOR AN AUTOMOBILE

*This blessing may be used upon newly acquiring a car or
upon preparing to take a long journey in it.*

Lord, Holy Protector and Source of All Blessings,
    we call down Your holy power of blessing
    upon this our automobile.

This machine,
    part of Your ever-unfolding divine creation,
    is to carry us on our journeys of life.
Bless it with Your protection
    and shield all who ride in it
    from harm and injury.
May those who drive it
    be ever mindful of its power for good
    and its power to harm.
May they be careful to drive with diligence
    and to show respect for Your gift of life
    by being aware of the rights and safety
    of all who use the streets and highways of the land.

Lord, help us to remember
    that this automobile is only a machine for travel;
    may we enjoy its wonder and its service
    without placing more importance upon its possession
    than what is intended.
May we treat it with proper care and respect
    as one of the many good things
    that You have given to us.

By Your grace, O Lord,
 may this possession of ours
 open doors in our lives
 for adventure, travel, beauty
 and service to others.
May You, our God,
 be our constant companion
 on our every journey.

May the blessing of Your divine name,
 Father, Son and Holy Spirit,
 rest upon this car and remain forever.

Amen†

Lord of Creation,
>who planted Your own garden called Eden,
>come and bless this soil
>which is to be our garden.

All that dies becomes earth,
>and so it lives again.
May this garden soil
>be both womb and tomb,
>a home for death and life,
>so that seeds of living things—
>of plants, of food and flowers—
>may die and resurrect
>here in our garden.

Ancient earth,
>our mystical mother,
>teach us, your children,
>that all things die
>to nourish life.

Gentle earth,
>be blessed with our love
>as we work in you.
Make us mindful that one day
>you will be our final bed
>of love and ecstasy.

Amen†

The garden may be sprinkled with water, and a simple cross of sticks or some other religious symbol may be placed in the soil.

Blessing Prayer
for Seeds

Water is needed with which to bless seeds (see top of p. 16).

Lord of All Life,
>who did hide Your Seeds in all that lives,
>be present here
>as we greet these tiny seeds
>with their gifts of life.

Seeds of life—so small,
>and yet, in the mystery of death and burial,
>you will produce life tenfold and more.

We sprinkle you with water,
>sacred sign of life,
>asking that you may be
>embraced by our mother the earth,
>fed by rain
>and kissed gently by the sun.

In caring for you
>we shall experience
>the most ancient profession of the human family,
>the primal vocation
>of being workers in the garden.

Soon you will be our pride and joy.

Soon you will be our food
>as you give up your life
>that we may live.

Seeds,
>pregnant with life,
>teach us the Easter secret of life,
>as we ask God to bless you.

Amen✝

Lord and Holy Creator of Trees and Forests,
    come and place Your blessing of life
    upon this (_____) tree
    that we are planting today.

In the Garden of Eden,
    You planted both the tree of knowledge
    and the tree of life.
May this (_____) tree
    be a tree of life to all the earth.
May its leaves breathe forth
    the life-breath of oxygen.
May its branches be living space
    for those who climb among them
    and for birds of the air that shall nest there.
May those in need of shelter from the summer heat
    find in its shade a refreshing refuge.
May it give to all who look upon it
    the gift of life-renewing beauty.

Lord, this our new tree
    is a stranger to us and we to it.
Remind us whenever we may pass by
    to make it feel at home
    by speaking to it with love,
    by greeting it with a song and a blessing.

May this tree's cousins in creation—
    other trees, grasses and wild flowers—
    welcome it and help it to recover
    from the shock of being moved.
As blessings, peace and life were the fruits
    of the tree of the Cross of Your Son, Jesus,
    may those same fruits flow from this (_____) tree
    which we plant in Your holy name,
    Father, Son and Holy Spirit.

Amen✝

29

BLESSING PRAYER AT THE COMPLETION OF THE HARVEST

Lord and Bountiful Creator,
    giver of grains and seeds, of fruits and berries
    and all that grows from the earth,
    we thank You and we bless You for this year's harvest.
We lift up our hearts in gratitude for the sun,
    which, together with rain, wind and earth,
    worked in harmony to produce this bountiful harvest.

We are grateful to all those
    who labored in—together with—the earth
    so that this harvest time might come to fullness.
Lord, as Your Son, Jesus, knew: harvest is hard work!
Yet, it is also richly rewarding
    to see the fruit of our labor,
    to take pride in this completed harvest.

We thank You, our Lord and God,
    for Your protection and care in this season of
    harvest.
We bless You for the weather given to us for our work.
This harvest, Lord, was not without its difficulties;
    no harvest is,
    but we rejoice that those times of trouble
    did not prevent us from the completion of this task.
The sun smiled on us, the wind cooled us
    and the earth laughed as we caressed her skin,
    collecting the fruit of this harvest.

Come, Lord of the Harvest, Lord of Rejoicing,
    come and join us in our festive celebration.
May our joy at this harvest
    be a taste of the joy we shall share
    when we celebrate the final harvest of heaven,
    that day of days when all that You have begun
    will be matured to completion.
Blessed are You, Lord our God,
    who has given to us this harvest.

Amen†

O Supreme Spirit of Creation,
    from Your divine heart has come forth
    a parade of pastoral animals—
    sheep, cows, horses, pigs, chickens, fish and fowl—
    in such variety and in such beauty
    that we daily marvel at Your creative imagination.

We praise You, that even these creatures
    have been blessed by You
    with a purpose in Your plan of the universe.
You have blessed them with beauty
    and with instincts that obey Your natural law.
May these creatures be protected
    from all disease and harm.
May they grow to completion and maturity
    so as to serve the needs of others.

As some will soon surrender their life
    that we might have food and support,
    may they call forth from us
    a desire to share our life for others.
As we, with gentleness and love,
    care for these Your creatures,
    may the food that they will provide
    be free of all that is harmful
    and nourish us in mind, body and spirit.

Help us to be patient, Lord,
    when they are slow to follow our instructions.

Help us never to treat them as dumb animals
    or as mere objects for trade and profit.
Blessed are You, Lord our God,
        who did give us these creatures as companions,
        as a source of feasting and celebrating
        and also to provide us with daily food.
May Your holy care be upon these creatures which we bless
        in Your name: Father, Son, and Holy Spirit.

Amen✝

O Supreme Spirit of Creation,
   from Your sacred breath came forth
   birds and beasts, fish and fowl,
   creatures of such variety and beauty
   that we are continuously amazed
   at Your divine imagination.
These children of Yours
   have been blessed by You, their Creator,
   with simplicity, beauty and a cosmic purpose.

They have been blessed as well
   by our greatest grandfather, Adam,
   who in Edenland gifted each with its own name.
They have also been blessed with protection
   by our ancient ancestor Noah, patron saint of those
   who seek to preserve all that You have created.
Sheep and goats, donkeys and cows,
   doves and serpents, fish and birds of the air
   were blessed by Jesus, Your Son,
   by His being born in their company
   and by His making use of them in His teachings.

May we, in this holy pattern, now bless (name)
   by taking delight in his/her beauty and naturalness.
May we bless this animal
   with a Noah-like protection
   from all that might harm him/her.
May we, like Adam and Eve,

speak to this creature of Yours
with kindness and affection,
reverencing his/her life and purpose
in our communal creation.

May we never treat _(name)_ as a dumb animal,
but rather let us seek to learn his/her language
and to be a student of all the secrets that he/she knows.

May Your abundant blessing rest upon this creature
who will be a companion for us in the journey of life.

Amen†

BLESSING PRAYER
WHEN ABOUT TO
LEAVE ON A JOURNEY

Blessed are You, Lord our God,
> for You have created a wide and wonderful world
> in which we can travel.

We ask Your blessing upon us
> as we are about to leave on a journey.

Be our ever-near companion, O Holy Guide of Travelers,
> and spread the road before us
> with beauty and adventure.

May all the highways ahead of us
> be free of harm and evil.

May we be accompanied by Your holy spirits,
> Your angelic messengers,
> as were the holy ones of days past.

On this trip may we take with us
> as part of our traveling equipment
> a heart wrapped in wonder with which to rejoice
> in all that we shall meet.

Along with the clothing of wonder,
> may we have room in our luggage
> for a mystic map
> by which we can find the invisible meanings
> of the events of this journey—
> of possible disappointments and delays,
> of possible breakdowns and rainy day troubles.

Always awake to Your Sacred Presence
   and to Your divine compassionate love,
   may we see in all that happens to us,
   in the beautiful and the bad,
   the mystery of Your holy plan.

May the blessing of Your name, Father, Son and Holy Spirit,
   be upon us throughout this trip,
   and bring us home again in safety and peace.

Amen✝

The travelers may make a sign of the cross or share a kiss of peace.

Blessing Prayer for Others Who Are About to Leave on a Journey

Blessed are You, Lord our God,
    for You have created a wide and wonderful world
    in which we can travel.
We ask Your blessing upon (_names_)
    as they are about to leave on a trip.
May You, Holy Guide of Travelers,
    be their ever-near companion,
    spreading the road before them
    with beauty and adventure.
Free that road from harm and evil,
    and send as their escorts
    Your holy spirits, Your angelic messengers,
    who accompanied the holy ones of days past.

On this journey, may they take with them
    as part of their traveling equipment
    a heart wrapped in wonder
    with which to rejoice in all they shall meet.

Along with that clothing of wonder,
    may they have room in their luggage
    for a mystic map.
With the aid of this map,
    may they read the invisible meanings
    of the events of this journey—

of possible disappointments and delays,
of possible breakdowns and rainy day troubles.
Always awake to Your Sacred Presence
and to Your divine compassionate love,
they shall see in all that happens,
in the beautiful and the bad,
the mystery of Your holy plan.

addressing travelers:

May the blessing of the Father,
and of the Son
and of the Holy Spirit
be upon you throughout this trip;
may it shield you from all harm
and bring you home again in safety and in peace.

Amen†

*In blessing the travelers, a small cross may be traced on
their foreheads, or they may be given a kiss of peace.*

Thanksgiving Prayer for a Safe Return Home After a Journey

Lord, we are home again,
    and we lift up our hearts in a song of gratitude
    for the blessings of our journey.
Holy Guide of Pilgrims and Travelers,
    You have been our personal escort upon this journey.
We are grateful
    for all we have seen and experienced,
    for the beauty we have met,
    for the new places we have visited.

We are thankful, also,
    for the protection from harm and injury that was ours.
Your angelic care surrounded us
    as an invisible shield against evil and harm.
Your love for us
    is now a cause for prayer and gratitude.

Lord, it is good to be home again.
Our time away has opened our eyes
    to see our home and belongings
    with greater appreciation.
Since half of the pleasure of a journey
    is in the coming home,
    we take joy in our return.

May this joy
    be a taste of the happiness awaiting us
    when we finally come home to You.

In that final homecoming,
>   we shall feast upon the fullness of Your love
>   as we are surrounded by the affection of loved ones
>   who have returned to You before us.
We pause now
>   and, in silence, lift up our hearts in gratitude
>   for the pleasures of our trip
>   and the blessing of being home.

pause for silent prayer

Blessed are You, Lord of All Who Travel,
>   for Your holy and gracious care while we traveled
>   and for bringing us home safely again.

Amen†

THANKSGIVING PRAYER
FOR THE SAFE RETURN
OF OTHERS

Lord of Pilgrims and Travelers,
    we bless You and we thank You
    for the safe return of _(names)_ from their journey.
The highways of life are places of danger
    as well as the source of beauty and adventure.
We are grateful that You have shielded them
    from all harm and injury.

Your holy care went before and after them,
    granting them protection in danger
    and refreshment in times of weariness.
We rejoice with them
    in all the sights, sounds and other pleasures
    that came to them on their journey.

May the joy of their homecoming,
    the fullness of heart and expanse of spirit,
    be a taste of the happiness that awaits them
    in their finally coming home to You, their God.
May our prayerful gratitude
    foreshadow their reception by family and friends
    at their final homecoming in heaven.

Lord God of Mary and Joseph,
    You who gifted the holy parents with joy
    upon their return to Nazareth from their sojourn in Egypt,
    grant joy and blessings to _(names)_ at their return.

Blessed are You, Lord of All Who Travel,
    for bringing them safely home.

Amen✝

Prayer
for Protection in a
Time of Storm or Danger

A candle, around which the family has gathered for prayer,
is lit.

Lord and Holy Protector,
> like the disciples who were caught in their tiny boat
> in the midst of a mighty storm,
> we come together to seek Your help.

We are fearful as we are surrounded by danger.
We feel helpless and small
> before the great power of this perilous time,
> a power which is beyond our control.

While everything seems dark and dangerous,
> we place our trust in You, our Lord and God.

Sheltered here in our home,
> we are also shielded by Your love
> against all that might harm us.

We know that You hear all prayers;
> so we now, filled with confidence,
> lift up our petitions to You, our God.

pause for silent prayer

Lord,
> we fear for our home,
> for our lives and for all we hold dear.

Your sacred blessing is upon this home
> and upon each of us as well.

We are secure in the power of that blessing.
May the saving power of the Cross of Your Son, Jesus,
    encircle us and our home.
May all evil, all harm and injury,
    be repelled by that sacred sign.

May the light of this candle
    be for us a holy sign
    of Your Divine Presence that fills our home
    in the midst of this danger.

Lord and Creator of Storms and of Rainbows,
    be with us in this time of danger.

Amen†

A Rainbow Prayer, A Blessing Prayer After a Storm or a Time of Danger

Lord and Divine Protector,
    when Your trustful servant Noah came forth from the ark,
    after a long and difficult storm,
    he built an altar where he and his family
    gave praise to You, their God, for saving them.
Your holy rainbow
    was both a sign and a shrine
    for that prayer of gratitude.

We, like Noah and his family,
    come now to thank You
    for protecting us in a time of danger.
That danger has now passed,
    and we prayerfully give thanks
    that You, our Lord, have heard our prayers
    and have kept us safe within Your holy hands.
Our sacrifice
    will be this lifting up of our hearts
    in gratitude and in praise of You.
We thank You not only for safety from harm
    but for this opportunity to place all our trust
    in You, our Lord and Savior.
This peril, even with its dark danger,
    has been for us a source of renewed devotion
    and of dedication to each other and to You.

Lord,
>You are a God who brings forth good things
>from the dark times of life.

From that which is bad and ugly,
>You create a rainbow of the good and the beautiful.

We pause,
>and, in silence, thank You
>for Your protection and blessings
>in this danger that has passed.

pause for silent prayer

46 Blessed are You, Lord our God,
>who saves those who trust in You.

Amen†

Upon Hearing Good News

My Lord and my God,
    such good news has come today,
    and I am overjoyed with its bright message.
My heart is full to overflowing
    with gratitude to You
    who are the source of all good things.
Like a child, joy fills the whole of me,
    each cell is celebrating,
    each muscle is alive with delight.

My prayer has been that in all things
    I might do Your holy will,
    in the great as well as small events of my life.
I lift up my heart in thanksgiving
    that this blessing, by Your design,
    is to be part of my life-journey.
May I use this great blessing
    to bring me closer to You, my God,
    and the world closer to peace.

I am grateful, Lord of All Good Gifts,
    for all who have given me support
    with heartfelt prayer and encouragement.
May they be richly blessed
    with good things and with health.
May all whom I love
    share in the joy of this day
    and this happy moment.
May they and I
    never forget the great wonders of Your love.

Lord, I ask that this flame of joy
    ever illuminate my life
    and be a lamp unto my prayers.

Amen✝

---

*This is the prayer of a parent who may be temporarily separated
from the other partner by work, sickness or duty. It can be the
prayer of those who are separated by death or divorce as well.*

My Lord and Holy Companion,
    I am alone in the awesome task of making a home.
I ask Your holy help
    to show me how to take on the responsibilities
    of both mother and father.
Direct my heart
    so that I may dispense the qualities of both parents,
    of gentle compassion on one hand,
    of firm discipline on the other;
    may I transmit true tenderness coupled with true strength.

These twin talents of the masculine and feminine
    are both within me,
    but it is difficult, Lord,
    to balance their daily expression in our home.

The days are long and the nights lonely,
    yet, with Your divine support,
    the impossible will unfold as possible,
    and our home will be more than a house.

My efforts to be two persons
    find my time directed to a great degree
    toward the needs of others;
    yet I, as well, am in need of comfort and love.

Let my prayer,
    my Lord and Secret One,
    renew my energy
    and remind me that I am not alone.
For You, my Lord, are with me!

The pathway of tomorrow is hidden from me;
    perhaps it is just as well.
May the unknown future
    only cast me into deeper trust and love of You
    and fill my heart
    with love enough for two.

Amen†

BLESSING PRAYER FOR A MOTHER WITH CHILD

The prayer-blessing may be made by the husband, with family and friends gathered around.

O Lord of All Life, hear our prayer
    as we ask Your blessing upon Your daughter, (*mother's name*),
    who has been given the marvelous gift of life
    to bear within her body.

We rejoice in this gift
    and pray that this child, alive within her,
    may soon join us in the light of day.
May this child be healthy of body and mind
    and free of physical difficulties.
May both this child, now hidden from our eyes,
    and the mother
    be under Your divine care.
We pray now in silence for both of them.

    pause for silent prayer

    addressing mother:

May the Mother of our Lord, Mary,
    all the saints,
    and all holy women and holy mothers of past ages
    be with you.
May the gentle spirits of sun, wind and rain,
    the promise of spring,
    and the beauty of flowers

be your constant companions.
May the strength of our mother the earth
help you to carry this child
so that when that hour, hidden from the beginning
of time,
finally arrives,
this child of God may come forth into the world
wrapped in love, joy and peace.

May the blessing of God, compassionate as a Mother,
of God the Son and the Holy Spirit
rest upon you
and upon your child.

Amen✝

Father and all present may trace the sign of the cross on the
forehead of the mother.

Prayer Of Dedication
to a Life of
Perfection and Service

Lord God, You who know the secrets of our hearts,
    come now and fill me with the spirit of sincerity
    as I pledge myself to You
    and to the coming of Your kingdom.

Lord, I desire to serve You with all my heart,
    with all my soul and with all my strength.
I surrender myself to Your holy plan for me
    as I seek to be perfect as You are perfect.
May I strive for excellence
    in all the work of my hands.
May I strive to live within the spirit of holy poverty,
    living a simple way of life.
May my greatest possession be Your love
    and the love of those around me.
I strive for excellence in loving,
    asking that my love be always chaste and whole.
May I strive to be obedient and open
    to the mystery of Your voice within me,
    willing to embrace whatever You may ask of me.

Lord and Friend,
    I rededicate myself
    to a life of prayer and worship of You.
May a song of praise be the constant melody of my heart.
I re-commit myself

to serve the needs of those around me
and the needs of all the world.
May I find my salvation *here*
at this time and in this place where I now live.
May my union with those who share my commitment
be a source of confirmation and inspiration to me.

Lord, I marvel that You, in Your divine wisdom,
have chosen me to be an instrument
of Your creative salvation.
May all the work of my hands,
even my failings and stumblings,
be leaven to make that much desired Kingdom a reality.
Bless me now with Your abounding love
as I promise to be Your friend, servant and holy minister.
May I ever live out this commitment,
in Your name: Father, Son and Holy Spirit.

Amen†

THANKSGIVING PRAYER AFTER A DEEPLY RELIGIOUS EXPERIENCE

At a worship service, retreat, marriage encounter, day of recollection, prayer meeting, time of renewal . . .

From the center of my being, I praise You, my Lord and God,
    for the beautiful experience that You have given me.
This time has enflamed my heart, renewed my dreams,
    and enabled me to see with eyes divine.
I heard Your ancient call
    within the words and events of this time now ended;
    Your call to personal holiness and perfection,
    the invitation to prayer and spirituality,
    the challenge of the Kingdom and the Church.

As the disciples of Your Son were set afire
    by Your Divine Spirit on Pentecost,
    this sacred time has encouraged me to greatness
    within the scope of my simple life.
I may soon forget the words that were spoken
    and the names of those who were involved,
    but what has happened has truly shaped my heart.

May the activities of my heart bear witness
    to the great grace of what has happened to me
    in the day to day world to which I return.

May this time of spiritual renewal
    become part of the fabric of my life;
    may it be part of a lifelong enrollment
    in the school of prayer.

May I build upon it with daily prayer,
    and with the discipline of my spiritual life.
Nourished by prayer, reading, thought and action,
    may the seeds of this renewal time
    take root and flower forth
    in a life-song of glory to You, my Lord and my God.

Amen✝

BLESSING PRAYER
FOR A MARRIAGE BED

Lord and Creator of All That Is Good,
> You who have been known to prophet and saint
> by the simple name of Love,
> be with us now
> as we bless our marriage bed.

We rejoice that Your Son, Jesus, spoke of Your kingdom
> as a wedding feast of love and joy.

This bed which we share
> shall be a place of sleep;
> may it also be a place of love and joy.

Make it, Lord, a holy place
> that is overflowing with refreshment and tenderness.

Open our eyes to see it as sacred
> since within it we shall recommit ourselves,
> in love and hope, to one another.

Daily, Lord, open our eyes
> so that we might understand the marvelous mystery
> of how, in our mutual love for each other,
> we experience You, our God.

Send Your holy spirits of gentleness and affection
> to surround this marriage bed
> so that we who share it
> may find communion and healing within it.

May the dark spirits of resentment and selfishness
> be forever forbidden to nap here,
> and may only love, joy and playfulness
> be permitted to sleep with us.

We pray, then, that the rich blessing of Your divine name,
   Father, Son and Holy Spirit,
   descend upon this bed
   and remain here forever.

Amen†

BLESSING PRAYERS
OF
GRATITUDE
AND
PRAISE

A frequent and a fertile prayer expression in the spirituality of Jesus was that of the Berakhot benedictions or blessing prayers. These benedictions are brief, composed of no more than a couple of sentences, and always begin with the same words: "Blessed are You, Lord our God." An example of this type of Jewish blessing prayer is the benediction, or grace, said before eating bread: "Blessed are You, Lord our God, King of the Universe, who brings forth bread from the earth." These prayers are not acts of blessing God, since God does not need to be blessed; they are, rather, expressions proclaiming the holiness of Almighty God. So numerous and varied are they that they touch almost every aspect of daily life. Berakhot blessings exist for countless occasions in which we taste, smell, see and hear. The list of blessings includes a prayer for new clothing as well as one for a new day. These beautiful and brief prayers express rejoicing for arms, legs, sleep and for everything that happens, good or bad. As such, these prayers are forms of joyous thanksgiving for the gift of simply being alive.

Such blessing prayers surrounded and nourished the prayer life of our Lord. Today, however, within our own tradition, only a few, such as the blessing or grace before meals, remain in use. Yet, how necessary is this type of prayer in our lives. The ancient rabbis said that anyone who enjoys the pleasures of this earth without a blessing is a thief! Thanksgiving and the remembrance of God's redemption form the life-giving center of our Christian spirituality. This sense of gratitude should find expression not only in our celebration of the Mass, the liturgy of thanksgiving, but also in our awareness of such common gifts as the sunrise, a new pair of shoes, or even a hot shower!

An interesting aspect of these benediction prayers which have arisen within the Jewish tradition is the fact that they are placed in the present tense. To pronounce a blessing prayer is to be reminded that we are, today, in the middle of the divine flow of gifts. Being in the present tense, they remind us that creation did not happen long ago, but that it *is* happening, here and now. God is gifting us with fresh pears, beautiful rainbows, the aroma of autumn leaves and safety in a storm—all in the present moment. The mystery of God's love for us is all around us, alive and dynamic. Prayer, in the form of these blessings, is a beautiful albeit feeble attempt to respond to such a marvel.

Whenever we pray the benediction prayers, we are praying in the pattern of Jesus and His companions. When we pray in such a style, we become students of His spirituality of perpetual praise of the Father. Such a pattern is indeed a royal and holy way to heaven.

The blessing prayers that are found on the following pages are intended as a ground upon which you may develop a habit of frequent and earthy prayers of gratitude. They begin with the prayer phrase, "Blessed are You, Lord our God, who . . . ," and follow with an expression of whatever you are grateful to be experiencing. At any of the ten thousand places where God touches your life, you can respond with one of these blessing prayers. The benediction prayers are expanded into a reflective prayer of praise that may assist you in lifting up your heart to the Lord of Gifts. These prayers may be used as part of the meal-table ritual, as part of the praise in morning and evening prayer or used simply in thanking God for some blessing or gift.

No more holy habit could be acquired than to let such prayers come to our hearts and lips spontaneously. Their creative use is left to your own imagination and originality. May these benedictions be an aid to the growth of your personal holiness and a prayer to usher you into the mystery of the Holy Eucharist.

BLESSED ARE YOU, LORD OUR GOD, WHO IN THE RICHNESS OF YOUR DIVINE LOVE, BLESSES US WITH GOOD THINGS.

Lord God, we bless You
    and are filled with gratitude for the numerous gifts,
    the countless blessings,
    that come to us from You.

Your blessings come in times of joy,
    in times of victory, in success and honor,
    and they come as well in times of pain and sorrow,
    in sickness and defeat.
Your blessings, however, come always as *life*.

We take pleasure in the fruit of Your creation,
    in the earthen blessings
    of fish and bird, tree and flower,
    each the harvest of Your divine heart.

We take delight in our eyes,
    in our ears, arms and legs.
We find joy in holidays and vacations,
    and in our work as well.
We thank You, Lord of Gifts,
    for friendships, family and fun.

In winning and in losing—
>   in being last as well as first—
>   we take relish in the challenge and adventure
>   of Your great gift of life.
Lord, we thank You for all the gifts
>   that flow fully, day and night,
>   into our lives.

Today, with full hearts,
>   in the company of Jesus, Mary
>   and of all Your saints,
>   we bless You for all the good that has come to us.

Blessed are You, Lord our God,
>   who in the richness of Your divine love,
>   blesses us with good things.

Amen✝

BLESSED ARE YOU, LORD OUR GOD, WHO HAS FILLED CREATION WITH LIGHT AND SPLENDOR.

Radiant Lord,
> we rejoice with hearts filled with gratitude
> that You are not a hidden God
> for You reveal Yourself daily
> through the mystery of light.

Your majesty and glory
> shine out from within all of creation,
> as well as from sun, moon and stars.

We walk by their light,
> and we also feed upon that light
> as it is transformed daily into our food.

Blessed are You, Illuminator of All Creation,
> for the gifts of sunrise, high noon and sunset.

In the splendor of the sun,
> the sky-wheel of energy and light,
> we see Your splendor, O Light of Lights.

Your Son, Jesus, called Himself
> the light of the world
> and invited us to be His luminous brothers and sisters
> and Your children of light.

We are grateful for the daily light of insight,
> that gift by which we see our way to You.

We are also grateful for shadows and nightfall
    which serve as background for this light.
In our lives, we often stand
    in the darkness of failings and suffering.
May Your Divine Light
    penetrate the murky overcast of these times,
    and radiate outward from the horizon of our hearts.
May Your Divine Presence
    be a shining star in the midst of gloom.

Like the plants of the earth,
    may we lean toward You,
    Eternal Source of All Light and Energy.
Help us, this day,
    to *be* light to all we meet.

Blessed are You, Lord our God,
    who has filled creation with light and splendor.

Amen✝

BLESSED ARE YOU, LORD OUR GOD, WHO DAILY GIFTS US WITH THE RISING SUN.

We sing praises this day, Lord and Creator,
for the day star, our sun,
which turns the frozen night of space
into life for all that share this earth.
The light of the sun heats our planet,
gives energy to plants and animals
and delights us with yellow waves of light and warmth.

Down through time,
holy men and women have become children of the sun
by warming with love all that was around them,
and thus did they become symbols of Your Light.
We are grateful for these persons of light,
for Moses, Isaiah, Ruth and Rebekah,
for Francis of Assisi (and _patron saint_),
for Joan of Arc and Teresa of Avila,
as well as for holy Mary, the Mother of our Lord.
For these persons
and for all those who, by their lives,
have led us from darkness to the light, we give thanks.

Most of all, we are grateful for Your Son, Jesus,
who continuously calls us to _be_ light
to each other and to the world.

He, who challenged the darkness of death upon a cross
and was victorious in the sunrise of His resurrection,
calls us, today,
to follow His journey of light.

May the sun dance upon our roof this day;
may we rejoice in the sacrament of sunny splendor
and feel Your divine warmth.

Blessed are You, Lord our God,
who daily gifts us with the rising sun.

Amen✝

Blessed Are You, Lord Our God, For the Wondrous Gift of Sight.

Creator God, Holy Parent,
    we thank You for all of our so often unnoticed natural gifts.
We rejoice especially, now, in our eyes,
    these two tiny but marvelous gifts
    that add so much to the fullness of our lives.
This gift of sight enlarges the world of our enjoyment
    and magnifies our appreciation of nature,
    of great works of art, of the gifts of books and printing,
    of those persons we love,
    and for this we are grateful.

We thank You, also, for the gift of insight
    by which our spirit sees and understands.
For the gift of the third eye,
    the eye of the heart,
    by which we may "stand-under" the meaning of life,
    we are indeed grateful.

We are especially thankful for Your Son, Jesus,
    star-born prophet, whose very coming
    was a healing light to the world,
    who opened the eyes of the blind
    and gave to a weary world *new sight*.
Blessed be all those who have taught us to see:
    prophets, poets, writers and movie-makers,
    friends and lovers, all teachers of vision.

May our eyes bless You this day;
    may they be opened-prayers of gratitude,
    as we attempt to overcome today any blindness of heart
    and any dullness of appreciation of the wonder of sight.

In the fullness of our being,
    we bless You, Incomprehensible Lord,
    who foresees a heaven of such splendor,
    that ear has not heard nor eye seen
    such beauty as You have prepared.

Blessed are You, Lord our God,
    for the wondrous gift of sight.

Amen✝

BLESSED ARE YOU, LORD OUR GOD, FOR THE GIFT OF HEARING.

In the fullness of our persons, we praise You, Lord our God,
   because You are a God of ten thousand gifts.
We are grateful, in this prayer,
   for the marvel of hearing
   by which we can know the songs of creation,
   Your unending melody of beauty,
   expressed in words, wind and whispers.
With open ears,
   we take in the joy of music,
   the delight of poetry
   and the simple songs of daily life.
For all of these blessings, we are filled with gratitude.

We rejoice that You have given us a third ear,
   the ear of the heart, the ear of the soul,
   with which we may listen to silent sound,
   to the silent music of Your divine heart.
Help us, Lord,
   by quiet prayer and times of silence,
   to open that third ear
   and to heal the other two of all noise.

We are also thankful
   for those persons who teach us how to listen:
   for poets, musicians,
   parents, prophets, and teachers.

Grateful are we, for that long line of holy people
from the East and the West,
who teach us to listen
for the echo of Your divine voice
in all words of truth.
For Your powerful yet gentle Word, Jesus,
whose Good News cleanses our ears,
we are especially thankful.

With listening hearts and grateful prayers
we adore You, Divine Master.

Blessed are You, Lord our God,
for the gift of hearing.

Amen✝

BLESSED ARE YOU, LORD OUR GOD, WHO DELIGHTS US WITH THE WONDER OF WIND.

Father of Ten Thousand Gifts,
    we are grateful for the invisible wonder of wind,
    for that playful spirit of nature
    that drives kites heavenward,
    carries away balloons on invisible fingers
    and twirls windmills joyfully.

We rejoice in this marvel, the wind,
    bearer of seeds, waver of flags and banners,
    carrier of clouds and sea-spray
    and messenger of God: as holy wind, the Holy Spirit.
We rejoice in that Holy Spirit
    who surrounded Mount Sinai with wind, smoke, and fire
    when holy Moses met You face to face.

For the breeze which held the voice of God
    that called Elijah from his cave of hiding,
    for the wind upon which rode the tongues of fire
    that came upon Jesus' friends after His ascension to You,
    we are grateful.

For all these gifts of the wind,
    the dance master of yellow leaves
    and bringer of spring rains,
    for the wind itself which we feel upon our bodies,
    we are thankful;

and we praise You, Spirit Supreme,
by enjoying on this day
Your holy creature and sacred singing sign,
the wind.

Blessed are You, Lord our God,
who delights us with the wonder of wind.

Amen✝

BLESSED ARE YOU, LORD OUR GOD, WHO FROM OUR MOTHER THE EARTH DOES DAILY GIVE US BREAD TO EAT.

In a gloria of gratitude,
>we are made mindful of the many marvels of life
>that spark our hearts.

You have not only given us life
>but continue to increase that life by nourishing us.

Blessed are You, Holy Sustainer,
>for the marvel of food,
>for bread and wine,
>for banquets and dinners, for picnics and suppers.

With compassionate love
>You fed Moses and his people in the desert,
>and You sustain us, today, with daily manna
>at breakfast, lunch and dinner.

We are thankful for Your Son, Jesus,
>who was the *living bread*
>broken, shared and eaten in love.

For this holy bread
>who calls us, each, to share ourselves unselfishly
>as food for one another,
>we bless You, Divine Source.

We take delight,
>with Moses, Jesus and all the holy ones,

that parents, friends, teachers and poets,
artists, musicians and people of prayer
have all been food for us.

Blessed are You, Boundless Father,
who have shared with us the secret of life:
to *become* nourishment and life
for each other.
May each meal we eat
be a wonder of worship of You.

Blessed are You, Lord our God,
who from our mother the earth
does daily give us bread to eat.

Amen†

BLESSED ARE YOU, LORD OUR GOD, WHO GIVES TO US NOURISHMENT IN TIMES OF SILENCE AND SOLITUDE.

From uplifted hearts, hearts full of gratitude,
    may this prayer of thanksgiving rise to You,
    God of All Gifts and of Great Generosity.
We are thankful for times of stillness
    which allow us to listen
    to that holy river of prayer
    flowing in the heart;
    for the presence
    of Your Holy Spirit within,
    the Spirit who prays continuously.

These times of quiet heal us, within and without,
    replenish our spirit with new strength
    and prepare us to meet the constant struggle of daily life
    with renewed hope and joy.

Like Your Son, Jesus,
    who climbed mountains at night,
    who retreated deep into the desert
    to find You in stillness,
    may we,
    after this silent-solitary communion with You,
    allow our lives to reveal
    Your glory and grace.

Lord, may the seeds of the tree of stillness
    bear fruit for us
    and for all the restless world.

Blessed are You, Lord our God,
    who gives to us nourishment
    in times of silence and solitude.

Amen✝

BLESSED ARE YOU, LORD OUR GOD, WHO HAS GIVEN TO EACH OF US A PERSONAL DESTINY AND PURPOSE IN LIFE.

76　We thank You, God of Mysterious Ways,
　　　　that You have a holy design
　　　　for each of us.
　　We rejoice
　　　　that we are, each of us,
　　　　special to You,
　　　　that our names are written in the palm of Your hand
　　　　and our place in history,
　　　　our purpose for existing,
　　　　is known within Your heart,
　　　　since endless ages.

　　We are grateful
　　　　for that long line of holy people,
　　　　who since ancient times have inspired others
　　　　by their faithfulness
　　　　to their own special destinies.
　　They, by their very lives,
　　　　shout out to us
　　　　not to compromise our destinies,
　　　　but to live fully within Your eternal design.
　　Blessed are You, Inscrutable Lord,
　　　　for those events, persons, talents and loves

which have helped us to discover adventure and purpose,
fruitfulness and meaning,
in our sometimes empty
and seemingly insignificant lives.
Blessed are You
for teachers, parents, and other guides
who call us out
from the cocoon of comfort and contentment
to embark upon that unique path
which You have set forth
for each of Your sons and daughters.

Blessed are You, Lord our God,
who has given to each of us
a personal destiny and purpose in life.

Amen†

BLESSED ARE YOU, LORD OUR GOD, WHO HAS MADE US FREE PERSONS.

With joyful hearts uplifted in gratitude,
    we rejoice in that freedom
    which each of us has been given.
We are a free people
    since we have come forth from the God of freedom.
We are a free people because we have worked to remain free
    of all that threatens to make us slaves.

We are filled with thanksgiving
    that You, our Redeemer,
    have shown us how we might be free
    in spirit and in heart as well as in body.

As You directed Your holy servant Moses
    to lead Your children Israel from slavery,
    from the oppression of Egypt,
    so continue to direct us
    so that we may stay free from the oppression of evil,
    of greed and the lust for power over others.

As free sons and daughters of God,
    may the lamp of truth burn brightly in our home
    and in each of our hearts.
As brothers and sisters of Jesus,
    may we be faithful, as was He,
    to the wondrous freedom of the children of light
    and be ever grateful for the pleasures of liberty.

May our profound reverence for truth,
    as piercing as a sword
    and ever-liberating,
    be our burning torch of freedom
    and our shield against enslavement.

Blessed are You, Lord our God,
    who has made us free persons.

Amen✝

BLESSED ARE YOU, LORD OUR GOD, WHO DAILY GIFTS US WITH TIME.

You who are Lord and Creator of Space and Time
     yet who lives beyond them,
     we praise You and honor You
     for the gift of minutes, hours, days and years.
Each second of life that You give
     is precious and profound.
We pause now so as not to take these gifts for granted—
     so that we may remember in a holy way
     that all time is holy,
     a gift which calls forth
     songs of gratitude from our hearts.

We pause to gratefully remember
     those holy persons of ages past
     who call us to measure time in a godly way.
We call to mind:
     Noah, counting forty rainy days and nights,
     Job, waiting with longing in prayerful patience,
     and Mary of Nazareth, numbering her nine months.

For those persons today who call us
     to take time for work and for play,
     to make time for love and praise,
     to create time for rest
     and the leisure necessary for creation,
     we lift up our hearts in thanks.

We who live in the present
    recall the past
    so that by our remembrance
    we might more fittingly prepare
    for the future time.

We who stand in the middle
    of a trinity of time—
    past, present and future—
    do bless You, Source and Sustainer of All Seasons.

Blessed are You, Lord our God,
    who daily gifts us with time.

Amen✝

BLESSED ARE YOU, LORD OUR GOD, WHO ENHANCES OUR LIVES WITH WORK.

For the gift of work, we are grateful in this prayer.
As the sons and daughters of Adam and Eve,
we follow in the steps of our first parents
who, before their fall,
worked joyfully with their hands
in Your Garden of Eden, Lord and Creator.

We are thankful for the dignity and creative challenge
of our unique tasks.
For the work that ennobles us,
that lifts up our spirits,
we are grateful.
By means of these labors,
we are able to give flesh to our spiritual dreams
and to work out the salvation of the earth.

We take time to thank You
for those common tasks that we must perform each day,
those necessary labors of life
by which, according to Your divine plan,
we are also able to create the Kingdom here in our midst.

We daily follow in the footsteps of Jesus,
the carpenter of Nazareth,
and in the way of Mary, His mother,
who gracefully worked at the tasks of her home,

82

as we rejoice in the opportunities for work
that form us in Your love.
With St. Paul, the tent-maker,
with St. Peter, the fisherman,
we too labor in love
as we proclaim the mysteries of Your Gospel of good news.

Help us, Lord our God,
to use the work of this day—
to perform it with mindfulness and attention,
with care and devotion—
that it will be holy and healing
for us and for all the earth.

Blessed are You, Lord our God,
who enhances our lives with work.

Amen†

BLESSED ARE YOU, LORD OUR GOD, WHO GIVES SPICE TO LIFE WITH CHANGE.

Lord and Source of All Gifts,
    we rejoice in the fullness of Your holy generosity.
We thank You especially now
    for the gift of change,
    that gift of newness
    that opens doors closed by habit and routine.

We bless You and thank You as well
    for that which is stable and unchanging,
    for the ancient and traditional
    which give meaning to the new and different.

We thank You, O End of All Longing,
    for the capacity for change in our lives,
    for without change
    there can be no real growth
    and no true life.

We are grateful, in this prayer, for those persons
    who, through their gifts of excitement and adventure,
    have taught us not to fear change,
    not to resist the new.
We are thankful for Your Son, Your Sacred Word,
    who spoke to us of new wine for new wine skins
    and who calls us daily
    to a new kingdom
    and to a new covenant.

May our hearts be ever-changing,
    ever in growth,
    as we journey to You, our Mysterious Source,
    You who are forever fresh and new
    yet forever the same.

Blessed are You, Lord our God,
    who gives spice to life with change.

Amen†

BLESSED ARE YOU, LORD OUR GOD, WHO GIVES US BIRTHDAYS AS TIMES OF JOY.

With joyful hearts and lighted candles,
    we praise You, O Lord of Time,
    as we are grateful for holidays and festivals,
    for birthdays and anniversaries.

This special day, like its sister celebrations,
    becomes a holy center around which we gather
    to celebrate the mystery of Your divine presence,
    which we call life.
Smile upon us who are born of Your eternal seed,
    as we praise You with prayer.

We thank You for parents,
    grandparents and great-grandparents:
    all the way back in history to Adam and Eve.
By this celebration of the anniversary of birth,
    we proclaim You as the holy center
    around which all life dances and celebrates.
Blessed are You, Sustainer of All,
    who has given to us Your ever-green,
    Your ever-life-full and never-dying seed.

With bird-song and wind-whisper,
    with waving grain and bowing branch,
    with candle flames and festive food,
    we bless Your holy name.

Blessed are You, Lord our God,
    who gives us birthdays as times of joy.

Amen†

BLESSED ARE YOU, LORD OUR GOD, WHO INVITES US TO BE HOLY FOOLS.

Father and God of Fools,
Lord of Clowns and Smiling Saints,
we rejoice that You are a God of laughter and tears.
Blessed are You, for You have rooted within us
the gifts of humor, lightheartedness and mirth.
With jokes and comedy, You cause our hearts to sing
as laughter rolls out from us.

We are grateful that Your Son, Jesus, the master of wit,
daily invites us to be fools for Your sake,
to embrace the madness
of Your prophets, holy people and saints.
We delight in that holy madness
which becomes medicine to heal the chaos of the cosmos
since it calls each of us
from the humdrumness of daily life
into joy, adventure
and, most of all, into freedom.

We, who so easily barter our freedom
for illusions of honor and power,
are filled with gratitude that Your Son, by His life,
has reminded us to seek only love,
the communion with each other and with You,
and to balance honor with humor.
With circus bands and organ grinders,
with fools, clowns, court jesters and comedians,

with high spirited angels and saints,
we too join in the fun and foolishness of life,
so that Your holy laughter
may ring out to the edges of the universe.

Blessed are You, Lord our God,
who invites us to be holy fools.

Amen✝

BLESSED ARE YOU, LORD OUR GOD, WHO GIFTS US WITH THE JOYS OF FRIENDSHIP.

With hearts filled with gratitude,
    we thank You, Lord our God,
    for gifting us with good friends.
We are grateful for all those persons in our lives
    who have chosen us to be their friends
    (and especially for _name_);
    for truly this is a rich and sacred trust.

By the sacrament of friendship,
    we share our mutual journeys to You,
    Source of All Love and Life.
In sharing,
    we find our happiness expanded
    and our sorrow lightened,
    and, for this blessing,
    we are indeed grateful.

We prayerfully rejoice
    that Your Son, Jesus, has called each of us
    from the position of servants
    to the honor of being His friends.
We are grateful for the numerous opportunities
    to express that honor in our lives with each other
    and in our prayer with Him to You.
May this thanksgiving
    season all our present friendships
    as it opens the doors of our hearts to new ones.

Blessed are You, God of Unity,
    for entering our lives through friendship.
Make us, we pray, worthy of such a gift
    by being faithful but non-possessive,
    by being loyal but honest
    and by being ever grateful
    for the gift of good friends.

Blessed are You, Lord our God,
    who gifts us with the joys of friendship.

Amen✝

Blessed Are You, Lord Our God, Who Crowns Marriage with Love and Affection.

Lord of Love,
    we thank You for the numerous gifts
    of our married love.
With the wisdom of generosity
    laid open since Creation,
    You have blessed the union of man and woman
    with deep beauty in the song of love.
A mystic melody of sacred unity
    arises when two hearts are fused as one
    in the love of the Eternal One.
Lord God, we thank You for this holy gift.

Lord and Creator of Life,
    Your loving union with Your people
    was sung by the ancients
    in symbols of wedding feasts and intimate unions.
No other vocation in life
    have You, Lord, so richly blessed
    by interlacing intimacy and affection
    in the sacred union of hearts and bodies.

We who share this ministry of marriage
    must also share its heavy burdens.
But our moments of loving affection,
    so human and so holy,

lighten our trials and nourish us day by day
in our common journey to You,
our Lord and Beloved.

Lord,
may the happiness of these times of tenderness
be for us a sacrament
of our future and endless unity
with You, with each other, (with our children,)
and with all Your holy saints and lovers.

Blessed are You, Lord our God,
who crowns marriage with love and affection.

Amen✝

BLESSED ARE YOU, LORD OUR GOD, WHO HAS GIVEN TO US HOLY PARENTS.

Lord of Life,
we are grateful for the gift
of parents, grandparents and great-grandparents.
These persons, who were chosen by You for us,
have shared with us not only life
but a multitude of gifts and talents as well.

We are each indeed homemade,
and our parents were the doorway
by which we entered into the wonder of life.
In our grandparents, we have sensed and felt
the thread of history and the treasure of tradition
that lays within our family.
We ask that those who guided our early steps
and called forth our latent talents
may be richly rewarded
by You, their Divine Parent.

In the long tradition of holy parents,
of Abraham and Sarah, Isaac and Rebekah, Jacob and Rachel,
may our parents be blessed
by Your faithful love.

May all teachers, guides and friends
who have, at times, been parental-persons to us,
be blessed as well
by Your divine compassion and care.

Show us, O Lord,
    how we can express our gratitude
    to those who have given us life
    by living lives of Light and Life.

Blessed are You, Lord our God,
    who has given to us holy parents.

Amen✝

BLESSED ARE YOU,
LORD OUR GOD,
WHO HEALS US WITH
FORGIVENESS.

With a healed and happy heart,
    we proclaim our thanksgiving to You,
      God of Compassion and Great Kindness.
We rejoice in Your absolution of our failings
    and in the fact that You call us
    to forgive each other daily
    with the sacrament of understanding,
    for in that mutual forgiveness,
    we experience Your divine grace.

We are grateful for those persons in our lives
    who have allowed us to be reconciled
    after we have become separated from them
    through selfishness and thoughtlessness.
For the numerous experiences of absolution in our past lives,
    for the lifting of the burden of guilt,
    we are thankful.

We are most grateful as well, Loving God,
    for the gift of Your Son, Jesus,
    who calls us to lives of compassion,
    to forgiveness and understanding.
He, by His life, gave us an example
    of how we are to love those who harm us
    and forgive those who injure us
    when He asked You, His Father,

to forgive those who had led Him to suffer
and die on a cross.

Teach us, Lord,
how to forgive ourselves
and to be patient with the slowness
of our growth in holiness.
Able to forgive ourselves,
we shall be more eager and able to forgive others
according to Your divine pattern.

Blessed are You, Lord our God,
who heals us with forgiveness.

Amen✝

BLESSED ARE YOU, LORD OUR GOD, WHO HEALS US AND RESTORES US TO LIFE.

Lord of Life,
>> we are grateful for the wholesomeness of life
>> and for the gift of good health.

Aware of the unity of body and spirit,
>> we affirm our constant need for their harmony
>> if we are to enjoy true health.

We are grateful for the marvels of medicine,
>> for doctors and nurses,
>> for all those who possess a healing touch
>> and practice the art of healing.
We are thankful for the way in which
>> our own bodies work to constantly heal themselves,
>> restoring us to the state of health.
We acknowledge that we have been healed
>> of depression and gloom
>> by laughter and affection,
>> healed of inner-injury by the medicine of forgiveness;
>> and for these times we are grateful as well.
We thank You for the ways
>> that beautiful music and silence heal our ears,
>> for the ways that color and form heal our eyes
>> and for how the magic medicine of make-believe
>> binds up the wounds of our broken dreams.

As we rejoice in Your gift of health,
 may we be ever-mindful of those
 who are steeped in Your gift of sickness
 as part of the divine mystery of salvation.

We thank You for the presence in our lives
 of Your Son, Jesus,
 who moved among us as both teacher and healer.
In the ancient tradition of the prophets,
 He heralded and also healed—
 both body and spirit—
 in Your Sacred Name.

Blessed are You, Lord our God,
 who heals us and restores us to life.

Amen†

Blessed Are You, Lord Our God, Who Watches Over Us In Times of Trial and Danger.

Thanksgiving fills our hearts,
    as we rejoice in You,
      our Lord and Holy Protector.
We who live in the midst of storm and sickness,
    of war and danger,
      who are daily exposed to evil of every sort,
      rejoice in Your constant
      and parental love for us.
Surrounded by darkness and the shadow of fear,
    we do not falter,
      for we trust that Your constant care
      cradles us
      and keeps us safe.

With angelic attention,
    You watch over our home
    and each of our bodily temples.
Your holy spirits surround us
    and, in winged wonder,
    call us to prayer
    and to confidence.

Guard us in this time of danger,
    as Your Holy Presence
    fills the darkness of this moment
    with the splendor of Your shelter.

Blessed are You, Lord our God,
    who watches over us in times of trial and danger.

Amen†

BLESSED ARE YOU, LORD OUR GOD, WHO SHARES PAIN AND SUFFERING AS PART OF THE MYSTERY OF LIFE.

Lord our God, Incomprehensible One,
    Your sacrament of suffering,
100   the mystery of pain,
    has burst into our lives.
We have been offered the cup of bitterness
    so that we may share in the sorrow of Your Son, Jesus,
    and so help to heal
    the sickness of our planet.

We thank You for this opportunity to explore,
    with those around us and with all the world,
    the puzzle of pain.
May we only seek the fullness of life,
    not rejecting the element of pain
    inherent in all growth
    and essential in each search for wholeness.

We, as disciples of Christ,
    follow in the footsteps
    of the Suffering Savior,
    asking that this pain
    have special meaning for us
    and for all the earth.

Blessed are You, Lord our God,
    who shares pain and sufferig
    as part of the mystery of life.

Amen†

Blessed Are You, Lord Our God, Whose Messenger Is Death.

Lord and Conductor of the Universe,
    we acknowledge and affirm the mystery
    of sunsets and farewells,
    of departures and finales
    as integral notes in Your divine chorus.
We are thankful even for the pains of daily dying,
    for the daily separations
    that are the counterpoint in our common lives.

With gratitude, we listen to the yearly song of creation,
    the melody of spring, summer and autumn
    which rises till the death-rest of winter,
    only to begin again in the evergreen resurrection of
        spring.
We take joy, as our hearts rise to You,
    that this divine harmony of death and life
    was sung by prophets and holy people,
    and that Your Son, Jesus,
    sang that song with His whole person
    in His death and resurrection from the tomb.

We are grateful for His living example,
    for Him who found it so difficult departing from
    His friends
    so that a greater experience of life
    might be His and theirs.
In His footsteps,
    along that path of death and resurrection,

we process toward our own death
and resurrection in You.
Help us, Compassionate God,
to let Your ancient and eternal song of death and
life
be played out in each of us,
as we live out our faith that death is but a doorway
that opens unto a greater and fuller expression of
life,
that opens to a final union with You who *are* life!

Blessed are You, Lord of life,
who alone knows the hour of our death
and ultimate union with You.

Blessed are You, Lord our God,
whose messenger is death.

Amen✝

HOLY DAYS
AND HOLIDAYS
OF THE
HOME CALENDAR

hurch calendars, which parishes customarily
make available at the beginning of the year, are
always a marvel of information. They list the
times of services for the parish, the names of the priests,
and, of course, the name of the mortuary that has spon-
sored the calendar. Hanging on the kitchen wall, decorated
with pictures from the life of our Lord or the lives of the
saints, they announce to the family the year's religious feast
days and fast days. Colorful signs and symbols indicate
changes in behavior or diet. The fish in Friday's space signals
abstinence, and the days of Lent and Advent are marked in
purple. Holy days have their special markers to ensure that
we take note of them. Oftentimes, in addition to this helpful
information, quotations of Scripture are printed in the daily
squares.

Often, on this religiously oriented calendar are scribbled
such personal reminders as "doctor's appointment" or
"Aunt Emma's birthday." Such reminders as these are insert-
ed into the list of special days that include Easter Sunday
and Ascension Thursday without defacing the calendar. Just
as the Church has her calendar of feasts, so each family
should have its own personal calendar that contains its special feast days of remembering. If we do not have a parish
calendar, then any calendar that provides some writing space

for each day can be used as the "official" domestic church calendar.

The keeping of such a calendar can be a means of helping us to celebrate life, opening to us a wide variety of opportunities to feast and to pray. These family feasts could include such special "remembering" days as birthdays, wedding anniversaries, the death days of parents and grandparents, the yearly days of remembering moving into the family home or burning the papers of a paid-off mortgage or the date of any event that has had a profound effect on the family. Each of these days may be the occasion for the family to gather for a special meal and for prayers. To the usual family table blessing could be added special blessings or prayers commemorating the particular event, and the meal could be enhanced by special foods and wine and highlighted with candles.

Such festive occasions that celebrate family history become a spiritual glue to strengthen the bonds of the family. If our holy household calendar reaches back to record such occasions as our parents' marriage date, the death dates of grandparents or parents or the baptismal dates of family members, it can give to all who use it a sense of family history and tradition. Celebrations of such personal feasts are roots that keep the winds of change from sweeping us away. Someone once joked that tradition for Americans was what they did last year! Indeed, as a nation and a culture, we are youthful. We lack the great and ancient traditions that are the pride of other societies. But in that lack is also hidden a touch of luck, for we can create our own traditions, even as a small family. From various lands and peoples, we can take those customs that speak to us personally and blend them into our home life. We have access to the great and enjoyable holy days of almost two thousand years of Christianity, which we may incorporate into our personal year of feasts. We may, if we so desire, also reach back to include some of the beautiful, rich and deeply spiritual feasts of Judaism,

mindful as we do that our Lord Jesus and His family celebrated these ancient holy days that recall God's compassionate care of His people Israel.

The opportunities for feast days and celebrations are as
varied as Valentine's Day and the Fourth of July and as different in tone as Mardi Gras is from the May Crowning.
These celebrations and especially the great feast days of the
Church such as Easter, Christmas and Pentecost should
always begin and find their completion within our family
celebrations of prayer and feasting. Regardless of how simple our home celebrations might be, we shall carry their
spirit to community Church celebrations. Doing so, we will
bring to the larger community the invaluable gifts of prayer
and rejoicing that form the basis for a vital parish.

The prayers and blessings on the following pages are
intended to provide a beginning for the creation of your
own celebrations of remembering. Indeed, blessed is our
God, who deepens our faith in our remembering.

> NOTE: *Since the family table is the central shrine, the cor-*
> *nerstone, of the domestic church, the prayers for the cele-*
> *bration of many of the high feast days of every home*
> *calendar will be found in the following section of this*
> *handbook, which speaks directly of the family table.*

Blessing Prayer
for a Birthday

Candles on the table or on a cake may be used in this blessing.

Lord of Life,
    as we celebrate this traditional feast
    in honor of the day when *(name)*
    was Your gift to her/his parents and to the world,
    we ask of You
    a blessing.

Bless *(name)* and each of us with wisdom,
    the wisdom that You shared with Your clever son,
    Pablo Picasso, artist and lover of life, who said:
    "It takes a long, long time for one to become
        young."

Make us younger
    on each birthday.
Awaken within us the child
    who is so often asleep with shame.
Open our eyes to wonder and awe;
    delight our hearts with amazement and playfulness.

candles may be lit

May candles burn bright on this feast,
    as signs of the fire of life
    that burns today, on this birthday, and on
        every day—

for all days and all eternity
in the heart of _(name)_
and in each of our hearts.

Lord of Birthdays and Festivals,
dance on our roof
and join us with Your divine mirth.
So be it.

Amen†

Holy Creator of the Gift of Life,
    we are joyful as we gather here
    to celebrate the birthday of *(name)*.
May all heaven join us as we feast and sing—
    saints and angels helping us to announce
    that *(date)* is a very special day.

addressing the birthday person:

May the real gifts of this birthday
    be the blessing of a long life and good health,
    the feasting and fun of our coming together
    and the love we all have for you.
Happy birthday, *(name)*,
    and may God bless you today
    and all the days of your life.

Amen†

BIRTHDAY BLESSING
PRAYER FOR A CHILD

Lord our God,
    not only (*name*) but each of us
    rejoices in this birthday
    because birthdays are among the best
    of all our family feasts.
Today we celebrate that (*name*)
    has been Your gift to all of us,
    a gift that grows more valuable in our hearts
    with each passing day.

Bless her/him on this her/his (*number*) birthday
    with blessings of good health,
    of laughter and happiness.
On this birthday, may her/his heart overflow
    with good things and beautiful dreams.

Lord, Holy Creator of Fun and Song,
    come and join us now as we wish (*name*)
    a happy birthday as we sing:

ALL SING: *Happy Birthday*

BLESSING PRAYER
FOR MOTHER'S DAY

This blessing could be given by the eldest child or by the father of the family.

God of Love,
> listen to this prayer.

God of Holy People,
> of Sarah, Ruth, and Rebekah;
> God of holy Elizabeth, mother of John,
> of Holy Mary, Mother of Jesus,
> bend down Your ear to this request
> and bless the mother of our family.

Bless her with the strength of Your spirit,
> she who has taught her child/children
> how to stand and how to walk.

Bless her with the melody of Your love,
> she who has shared how to speak, how to sing
> and how to pray to You.

Bless her with a place at Your eternal dinner table,
> she who has fed and nurtured
> the life that was formed within her
> while still helpless but embraced in her love.

Bless her today,
> now, in this lifetime,
> with good things, with health.

Bless her with joy, love, laughter,
> and pride in her child/children
> and surround her with many good friends.

May she who carried life in her womb
    be carried one day to Your divine embrace:
    there, for all eternity,
    to rejoice with her family and friends.

This blessing and all graces, we pray,
    descend upon the mother of our family:
    in the name of the Father,
    and of the Son
    and of the Holy Spirit.

Amen†

Family members may give a kiss or other sign of affection to the mother.

BLESSING PRAYER
FOR FATHER'S DAY

This blessing could be given by the eldest child or by the mother of the family.

Blessed are You, Lord and Father of All Life,
  who has given to us
   the gift of the father of our family.

Today, we honor him,
  and we thank You for the numerous good things
  that are ours because of him.
His love for us
  has been a sign of Your divine affection
  and a sharing in Your holy love.
His continuous concern for our needs and welfare
  is a mirror of Your holy providence.
And so, as we honor him,
  we praise You, Father of All Peoples.

Bless him this day
  with Your strength and holy power
  that he may continue to be a sign of You, our God,
  and a priestly parent to our family.
May we who have the honor of bearing his family name
  do so with great pride.
May we, the members of his family,
  assist him in his holy duties as a parent
  with our respect,

our obedience
and our deep affection.

Bless him, Lord,
with happiness and good health,
with peace and with good fortune,
so that he who has shared of his very life
may live forever with You,
his God and heavenly Father.

This blessing and all graces, we pray,
descend upon the father of our family:
in the name of the Father,
and of the Son
and of the Holy Spirit.

Amen✝

*Family members may give a kiss or other sign of affection to
the father.*

Blessing Prayer
for a Daughter

For any special occasion such as the first day at school, first Holy Communion, Confirmation, graduation or marriage.

FATHER: Lord our God, be with us now as we pray.
   Look with favor upon this our daughter, *(name)*,
   for whom today is most special and beautiful.
Her mother and I,
   together with all our family,
   surround her with our gentle love and prayer
   (as she prepares to _____).

   addressing daughter:

MOTHER: My daughter and flower of my womb,
   this will be a day for you to remember
   all of your life.
We, your family, are grateful
   that we are able to share it with you
   and are able to support you
   with our prayers and love.

FATHER: Blessed are You, Lord our God,
   who has graced our daughter with life and health
   so that she might reach this beautiful day.
You have blessed her with many graces over the years
   and have carefully prepared her
   for this important step in her life.

addressing daughter:

(*name*), we, your family, now pause
and, in silence, call down
the richness of God's blessing upon you.

pause for silent prayer

Lord our God,
bring together and unite
all our prayers, our hopes and love
into a single blessing for her.

addressing daughter:

As God blesses you, my daughter, with divine grace,
we bless you with our love,
in the name of the Father, and of the Son
and of the Holy Spirit.

Amen†

*Parents, children and guests may kiss the daughter or sign
her on the forehead with the sign of the cross. Father and
mother may impose hands upon her head in a special
parental blessing.*

For any special occasion such as the first day of school, first Holy Communion, Confirmation, graduation or marriage.

FATHER: Lord our God, be with us now as we pray.
    Look with favor upon this our son, (*name*),
    for whom today is most special.
His mother and I,
    together with all our family,
    surround him with our love and prayer
    (as he prepares to _____).

    addressing son:

MOTHER: My son and child of my womb,
    this will be a day most special to you,
    one that you will long remember.
We, your family, are grateful
    that we are able to share it with you
    and are able to support you
    with our prayers and love.

FATHER: Blessed are You, Lord our God,
    who has graced our son with life and health
    so that he might reach this day.
You have blessed him abundantly over the years
    and have carefully prepared him
    for this important step in his life.

116

addressing son:

(name), we, your family, now pause
and, in silence, call down
the richness of God's blessing upon you.

pause for silent prayer

Lord our God,
bring together and unite
all our prayers, our hopes and love
into a single blessing for him.

addressing son:

As God blesses you, my son, with divine grace,
we bless you with our love,
in the name of the Father, and of the Son
and of the Holy Spirit.

Amen✝

Parents, children and guests may kiss the son or sign him on the forehead with the sign of the cross. Father and mother may impose hands upon his head in a special parental blessing.

Baptismal Ritual in the Home (To Follow the Celebration That Has Taken Place in the Church)

Too often a line is drawn between the prayer and ritual which takes place in the church and the family celebration that follows in the home. One place seems to be for prayer and worship and the other for celebration. This service of both blessing and prayer is intended for parents who wish, with family and friends, to prayerfully reflect within the intimacy of their home upon the church's baptismal rite.

When all have returned from the church following the Baptism, the father of the child begins by addressing the guests and family who are present.

FATHER: Welcome to our home.
We ask that each of you join us
    as we pray for and bless our newly baptized child.

I announce to you, with great joy,
    that (*Wife's name*) and I
    have been given the marvelous gift of life.
We present to you
    and to all the peoples of this earth,
    our son/daughter who was born on (*date*),
    and whom today we have dedicated to God.
Our child has been washed in the holy waters of
    Baptism

and has been embraced as a member
of a wider and greater family,
the Family of God.
He/she has been united mystically
with our Lord, Jesus Christ.

His/her mother and I
have given to him/her this name, (child's name),
by which he/she shall be known.
May our child and this name
be enrolled forever in the Book of Life.

As parents, we ask your prayers and support

so that we may show him/her the path of life,
the holy way of Christ,
by our lives lived in love of God and one another.
May you his/her godparents
and all his/her brothers and sisters
likewise be good examples for him/her
by showing the way to live as a family united in God.

addressing child:

My son/daughter, I bless you
in the name of the Father, and of the Son
and of the Holy Spirit.
Amen✝

*The father traces a sign of the cross on the child's forehead
and then kisses the child.*

MOTHER: (Child's name), I, your mother,
bless you with tenderness
and call upon God to watch over you, my child,
all the days of your life.
You, (child's name), are the flower
of the love between your father and me.

Today, on this feast of your baptism into Christ,
we rejoice in your membership
in Him, our Lord and Savior,
and in the Family of God,
a world-wide and cosmic family.

We announce to all who are present and to everyone
that you, my child, have a holy purpose in life,
that you are a royal and priestly person.
For all eternity,
from before the dawning light of Creation,
God has known your name
and has held you as precious.
We rejoice, today, that this dream of God
has become flesh and blood,
has become our child.
Your father and I sincerely ask
all those who are present
for their prayerful support
so that we may encourage you, (child's name),
to become who you really are:
a unique and creative individual.
We pray that we may be
good and loving parents to you,
now newly anointed and baptized as a child of God.
I bless you, (child's name),
in the name of the Father, and of the Son
and of the Holy Spirit.

Amen✝

*The mother traces a sign of the cross on the child's
forehead and then kisses the child.*

GODFATHER: (Child's name), we rejoice in the honor
that has been given to us as your godparents
to have you as a child of the Spirit of God.

Your godmother and I
    ask God's special blessing for you,
    our child of the Spirit.
All children are God-children, but you
    will be a godchild to us in a most special way.
We pledge to you, before all who are here present,
    our assistance at those times in your life
    when we may be of help.

GODMOTHER: May our lives as your godparents
    be for you an example of faith,
    and of great hope and affectionate love.
We rejoice in this day
    as do your parents and all your family.
We look upon you as a gift from God
    and celebrate the fact that you are meant
    to bring beauty and grace into our world.

<u>(Child's name)</u>, all of creation—
    streams, mountains, birds and beasts,
    trees, flowers, oceans, and stars—
    are brothers and sisters to you.
May you learn to live in harmony with them
    and with all the members of the human family.

May the blessing of God surround you all your life
    as we now bless you
    in the name of the Father, and of the Son
    and of the Holy Spirit.
Amen†

*The godparents trace a sign of the cross on the child's
forehead and then kiss the child.*

*The following concluding prayer may be said by either of
the parents if other family or friends are present.*

PARENT: Family and friends,
we have shared in the baptism of this child
into the mystery of Christ and His Church.
As witnesses and concelebrants
of this ancient and sacred ritual of Baptism,
let us now pray in silence
for the needs of _(child's name)_.

pause for silent prayer

As prayerful witnesses of his/her Baptism,
I now invite all of you to come forward
and bless him/her with a gentle kiss
and with the sign of Christ's cross.

If grandparents are present, the prayer continues before others come forward.

Mindful of how life is passed from parent to child,
may the grandparents come forward
and give to this their grandchild
their most special and holy blessing.
(The other members of the family may follow
and then our honored and beloved friends.)

It would be fitting for a party or celebration to conclude this service of prayer.

Ritual Blessing
for an Engaged Couple

*The sacredness of marriage is reinforced by those impor-
tant ritual steps that lead to it. Engagement should be more
than a social act; it should also be surrounded by the beauty and the grace of God's blessing. The ideal celebrants of
such a blessing are the parents. If all four parents are not
able to take part in the blessing, then the roles may be divided among the parents who are present-or grandparents,
other relatives or even close friends may join in performing
the blessing. Appropriate changes in the prayer would then
need to be made to fit each person who is giving the
blessing.*

*The engaged couple, together with their parents, grandpar-
ents, family and friends gather in a family home for the formal announcement and blessing. Song and music may be
used as part of the blessing, and flowers and candles may
highlight the celebration.*

The couple's announcement of their engagement:

GROOM-TO-BE: With great joy we announce to you,
   our parents and friends,
   to our family and to all the community,
   our desire to be united
   in the lifelong commitment of marriage.
<u>(Partner's name)</u> and I do, in your presence,
   engage ourselves to one another
   in preparation for the sacred union of marriage.

BRIDE-TO-BE: We ask your blessing upon our
engagement
and your prayers so that we may best use this time
to grow in love and knowledge of one another.
We ask your love-filled support
so that we can be sensitive to one another's needs
and so achieve a mutual understanding
of our intellects, emotions and spirits.
Surround (*partner's name*) and me with your prayers
on this most special and holy day in our lives.

The parental blessing of the couple:

FATHER OF THE BRIDE-TO-BE:
(*name*) and (*name*), we, your family, rejoice
that you have found the great treasure of love,
and we gladly support you
as you spend these days of preparation for marriage.
(*Bride-to-be's name*), your mother and I remember with joy
that same beautiful time in our lives
and so are pleased to share your happiness.
We are truly proud of you as our daughter
and know that you will continue to be
a source of pride and love to us all our days.

If a ring has sealed the engagement, the father of the bride-to-be continues:

Lord, may Your blessing be upon this ring,
a symbol and sign of the promise of love
between (*name*) and (*name*).
May she who wears it
see in it an everlasting, unbroken sign
of Your divine love for all of us.
May this engagement ring
be a living sign and pledge
of their coming marriage to one another.

MOTHER OF THE BRIDE-TO-BE:

(name) and (name), I, with all your family,
    give thanks to God
    for the gift that you have been given
    and rejoice with you in your mutual love.
Know of my prayers for you
    during this your engagement period
    that it may be a time of great joy and rich blessings
    and also a time of mature discernment.
May you find the grace to lovingly and deeply explore
    the problems as well as the joys that may lie ahead
    so that you can freely take up and embrace
    a deep-rooted and lasting commitment of matrimony.

May, then, the fullness of God's blessing
    be upon you, (name) and (name),
    and enrich these days of engagement
    with affection, grace and peace.

FATHER OF THE GROOM-TO-BE:

(Groom-to-be's name), your mother and I rejoice with you
    that you have found in (bride-to-be's name),
    a woman that you can love
    and someone with whom
    you can share the rest of your life.
Know that we and all your family
    will support you with encouragement and prayer
    as you prepare for the day of your marriage.

Let us all pause and in silence
    pray to God for the needs of this couple.

    pause for silent prayer

addressing couple:

May the Lord of Love
    bless both of you on this day
    and on all the days of your lives.

MOTHER OF THE GROOM-TO-BE: (*Groom-to-be's*
    name), my son,
    your father and I take great pride in you
    and share your happiness
    in your love for <u>(*bride-to-be's name*).</u>
We pray that the happiness of these days of preparation
    will be a sign of the joy of your future marriage.
May God bless you with all the gifts you may need
    during this special time in your life.

Now that you have publicly declared
    your desire to be engaged
    and having been surrounded
    by the prayer and support of family and friends,
    I ask you now to seal this engagement
    with affection and a kiss.

Amen✝

    couple kiss

*After the blessing, each of the parents may embrace the
couple, followed by the grandparents, the rest of the family
present and friends. It would be fitting for the blessing to be
concluded by a feast and celebration.*

BLESSING PRAYER FOR RENEWING A COMMITMENT BETWEEN TWO PERSONS

At hand should be two partially filled (with wine or . . .)
glasses and a third glass, which is empty.

ONE: Holy Creator of Love,
  we celebrate and renew our mutual lives
  that are lived as one.
We reseal, by this holy prayer,
  our commitment to each other
  to a life of shared dreams, thoughts and feelings.
We ask Your holy help
  so that we may be always awake
  to the needs of each other,
  needs both spoken and unspoken.
May our two but twin pathways
  lead us to the fullness of life
  and to You.

OTHER: We ask Your divine protection
  from the strong tides of daily troubles
  that tend to pull us apart from each other.
Shield us from the social sickness of no commitment.
Show us how to rechannel
  the hidden streams of selfishness
  that always threaten to separate us.
Lord, it was said by the ancients
  that from each of us flows a light

that reaches straight to heaven;
that when two persons destined to be united
come together,
their two streams fuse into a single bright beam
reaching to heaven
and giving splendor to all the universe.
We ask that our love for each other
will shine as a single flame to all.

ONE: We thank You for the gifts of past years
as we place our hope in the ancient truth
that whatever is begun here on earth

will flower to fullness in heaven.
As a sign of our desire to be united,
today and in the days to follow,
we join now our glasses as one
and share a common chalice of our covenant
with each other and with You, our Lord and God.

Amen†

Each partner now pours from an individual glass into a third and empty glass. Each then drinks from this one ceremonial glass.

BLESSING PRAYER
FOR ONE WHO IS RENEWING
RELIGIOUS COMMITMENT

Lord our God, blessed are You
    who have invited _(name)_
    into a life of sacred service
    of You, of the Church and of all the earth.
God of Abraham, Moses, Ruth and Esther—
    and of all other holy people whom You have called
    to special life-tasks in Your service—
    bless, now, our sister/brother-in-Christ.
By living a dedicated life, she/he seeks
    the coming of Your kingdom here on earth.
We, who are fellow pilgrims
    on her/his journey to Your divine heart,
    rejoice today in her/his rededication
    to a life of holiness and service.

    addressing one making commitment:

May you, our sister/brother,
    find that your pilgrimage in life has special meaning
    because of the life you share with us.
May our separate but parallel pathways to God
    give you insight into your unique calling.
May happiness be yours;
    may your sorrows be brief
    and always a part of your growth in Christ.
May this celebration of renewal
    deepen within your heart

your dream of younger years,
the dream to be a holy person.
Enkindle again that holy passion
to be possessed by the Divine Presence
and to allow the fullness of God
to shine forth from within you.

We prayerfully ask this day
that God would fulfill in you, in part,
that divine promise of a hundredfold harvest
given to all those who would dedicate themselves,
body and soul,
to the work of the kingdom of God.

We bless you, <u>(name)</u>,
with affection and encouragement.

Amen✝

*The sign of the cross may be traced upon the person by each
one present, or the kiss of peace may be given.*

New Year's Blessing Prayer for Clocks and Calendars

Watches and calendars may be placed on the table

Lord, You who live outside of time,
    and reside in the imperishable moment,
    we ask Your blessing this New Year's Day (Eve)
    upon Your gift to us of time.

Bless our clocks and watches,
    You who kindly direct us
    to observe the passing of minutes and hours.
May they make us aware of the miracle
    of each second of life we experience.
May these our ticking servants
    help us not to miss that which is important,
    while You keep us from machine-like routine.
May we ever be free from being clock watchers
    and instead become time lovers.

Bless our calendars,
    these ordered lists of days, weeks and months,
    of holidays, holydays, fasts and feasts—
    all our special days of remembering.
May these servants, our calendars,
    once reserved for the royal few,
    for magi and pyramid priests,
    now grace our homes and our lives.
May they remind us of birthdays and other gift-days,
    as they teach us the secret

that all life
is meant for celebration
and contemplation.

Bless, Lord, this new year,
each of its 365 (366) days and nights.
Bless us with new moons and full moons.
Bless us with happy seasons and a long life.
Grant to us, Lord,
the new year's gift
of a year of love.

Amen✝

MARDI GRAS
TABLE BLESSING
(ON THE EVE OF
ASH WEDNESDAY)

Lord our God,
    on this eve of Ash Wednesday,
    we ask that You bless our celebration
    of the feast of Mardi Gras.
Bless our table, our food and wine,
    as well as all of us
    who sit about this feast day table.

Come, Gracious Lord,
    and join us at this feast
    as we prepare to join Your Son, Jesus,
    by prayerfully entering into
    these forty days of Lent.

As the food and wine of this feast
    give nourishment and strength
    to our bodies and spirits,
    so may we, during this coming season of Lent,
    give strength and support to each other
    and to all who accompany us
    on this pilgrimage of prayer
    from Ash Wednesday to Easter Sunday.

As this Lenten roadway causes us to reflect
    upon the death of our Lord,
    may we also remember His victory
    in His resurrection from the dead.

May this dinner
>on the eve of the day of ashes
>be a joyful foretaste
>of the rebirth and new life that is the promise
>of the feast of the Resurrection.

Together, for the final time before these forty days,
>let us sing the ancient song of joyful victory:
>Alleluia!

ALL SING OR TOAST: Alleluia!

BLESSING PRAYER
FOR THE FEAST OF ST. PATRICK
(MARCH 17)

*This blessing could be used at the main meal of the day on
March 17.*

Lord of All Nations and All Peoples,
  we rejoice today in a special servant of Yours,
  St. Patrick.
Irish or not, Catholic or not,
  we all dance a gleeful jig
  on this his joyous feast day.
Lord of bishops, bakers and bartenders,
  we thank You for sprinkling saints among us
  like holy Patrick, Bishop of Ireland.

His green feast day gives us all a chance
  to wear the green of spring and life.
Four days from now our old friend winter
  will loose his lease on life.
Packing up his ice and snow,
  his chilly winds and frosty breath,
  he'll soon be gone.
The green of this day
  foretells of rich vegetation
  soon to grace our countryside;
  proclaims the fresh and new
  to the tired and weary;
  announces to one and all
  that spring is on her way!

Glory for spring and saintly Patrick,
    whose feast of songs and jokes,
    of dancing feet and faerie folks,
    will be for us
    the eve of springtime.

As Patrick sent snakes slithering out of Ireland
    by Your blessed touch,
    may we, each, through his pastoral intercession,
    be freed of any evil in our lives.

Lord of All Seasons,
    winter is on his deathbed,
    but song and mirth are greening all around us.
Blessed be St. Patrick, bishop and man of prayer.
Blessed be all saints,
    and the wee folk as well.

Amen†

PRAYER
FOR THE BLESSING OF BREAD
ON THE FEAST OF ST. JOSEPH
(MARCH 19)

As well as being the patron saint of a happy death, of all workers, and of the universal Church, St. Joseph is the patron of the Christian home. It is, therefore, especially appropriate to commemorate his feast day with a blessing prayer in the home. It is the custom of many families of European and especially of Italian ancestry to bless St. Joseph's day bread—or, in Italian, Fritelli. This blessing is enriched if the loaves are homemade according to a traditional or special recipe, but the common bread of the meal may also be used. Because of St. Joseph's role in the holy family, it would be appropriate for the celebrant of this blessing to be the father of the family.

The prayer on these two pages may be said in its entirety; if a shortened version is desired, the blessing may begin with the section of the prayer found on the following page.

We honor you, St. Joseph, on this your feast day.
We praise you, husband of the Blessed Mother, Mary,
    and father-protector of the blessed home at
      Nazareth.
We ask you, this day,
    to be the patron-protector of our home as well.

We commemorate your feast with this St. Joseph bread,
    symbol of the sustenance
    which you gave to the holy family.
May God, the Divine Parent,

fill this bread with richness of taste
and with the delight of His grace.
As we honor you today, St. Joseph,
you who steadfastly trusted
that in your dreams and intuitions
you were being guided by the hand of God,
may we who share this bread
be fed with wisdom and insight
and be nourished by a more abundant trust in God.

May this bread provide us with the same gifts
that you, Joseph, gave to Mary:
the gifts of strength and understanding,
the gifts of compassion and love.
May we nourish and rejoice in one another
as we share in this blessed bread,
and may it be for us
a source of protection from all evil and harm,
just as you, Joseph, protected the child Jesus
from these and all dangers.
St. Joseph, you who are the patron saint
of the universal Church and of every Christian
home,
watch over this our domestic church
with your persevering and loving care.
May this bread, created in your honor,
be not only a cause of celebration,
but may it also be nourishment for us
throughout all our life journeys.
May it and your intercession sustain us
so that at the end of our days
we may be blessed with a happy death.

St. Joseph, we give you honor
as we ask that the blessing of God,
the Father, Son and Holy Spirit,
rest upon this bread and remain forever.

Amen✝

BLESSING PRAYER
FOR PENTECOSTAL WINE

Lord, Creator of the Good and the Beautiful,
    hear our prayer as we celebrate
    the great fiery feast of Pentecost.

On this day, nearly two thousand years ago,
    the apostles were enflamed by Your Holy Spirit,
    and their great zeal was mistaken
    for an overindulgence in other spirits.

Send forth, Lord, as we celebrate,
    Your Sacred Spirit over these creatures of Yours,
    the spirits of wine (and cider)
    so that they might be filled to overflowing
    with Your joy, healing and magic.

May this blessed wine of Pentecost
    be for us a sacred sipping sign
    of Your delicious and delightful Presence
    among us, Your people.

May this blessed wine
    bring friends closer to friends
    and transform the stranger into a friend.

May all who share this sacrament—in moderation—
    be released from the toil of daily work,
    healed of any dullness of heart
    and have their feet set a-dancing.

May these spirits of wine (and cider)
    be the toast of our celebration
    and the taste of the Holy Spirit among us
    as we bless them now
    in Your name: Father, Son and Holy Spirit.

Amen†

BLESSING PRAYER FOR THE GIFT OF GRAPES ON THE FEAST OF THE ASSUMPTION OF MARY

We praise you, Mary, the Virgin Mother of our Lord,
    on this your festival of the Assumption,
        the feast of your glorious reception into heaven.
We honor you, earth's mother and heaven's queen.
In venerating you,
        we give glory to God in our prayers of gratitude
        for the bountiful harvest of gifts
        that have come to us this summer season.
We rejoice in all the taste-full
        and colorful gifts of our mother the earth—
        in wheat, corn and all grains,
        in apples, plums, grapes
        and all the fruits of the land.
For these fruitful blessings of the earth
        and for all gifts,
        we are truly thankful.

With our Armenian brothers and sisters in Christ,
        who on this day make merry
        in a special and joyful celebration,
        we too rejoice in this year's harvest of grapes.
From the dawn of history,
        grapes have been a rich source of food
        and have been transformed
        into that blessed beverage, wine,

which has been a delight for the heart,
a bond for friendships
and a maker of magic at feasts and celebrations.
It has, further, been given the place
of being an essential gift
in our eucharistic worship of our God.

Through your intercession, O Holy Mother,
we ask a divine blessing
upon these grapes.
May all who taste them give God praise.
May all who eat them savor the joy of this feast.
We now enrich them with this blessing
in the name of the Father, and of the Son
and of the Holy Spirit.

Amen†

142

*The traditional Advent wreath consists of evergreen
branches formed into a circle with four candles represent-
ing the four Sundays of Advent. By custom, the candles are
purple, and often the candle for the third Sunday is pink as
a sign of rejoicing; however, any colored candles may be
used. Purple or other colored ribbons may also adorn the
wreath. This prayer is intended for a blessing of the
Advent wreath itself, and the prayer on the following page
may be used when lighting each of the candles.*

Lord, Source of All Energy and Light,
　　the ancients saw the sun
　　as a great fire wheel rolling across the sky.
May our Advent wreath, this small wheel of green,
　　be for us a symbol of the sun
　　and of the Son of God.
May its ever-greenness
　　be a sign of life and of light
　　in the midst of the darkness of winter.
May the candles that burn brightly upon it
　　remind us of Your Son, Jesus,
　　who was the light of the world.

Grant, Lord, that this our Advent wreath
　　may be for us and for all who visit our home
　　a sign of faith in a world grown cold with disbelief,
　　a symbol of hope in a time of gloom and despair
　　and a flaming image of love
　　in a winter of mistrust and hate.

May all who look upon this symbol of Advent
   be encouraged to prepare their hearts
   for the coming of our Savior, Jesus Christ.
May this green wreath with its bright candles
   help us to prepare for the real Christmas
   which happens within our hearts.

May, then, Your blessing—Father of Light,
   Son of Glory and Spirit of Love—
   be upon this Advent wreath and upon our home.

Amen†

BLESSING PRAYER
FOR LIGHTING A CANDLE
ON THE ADVENT WREATH

One candle is to be lit at the beginning of each of the four weeks of Advent. A child may well be allowed to light the candle while the prayer is being recited.

Lord God,

    You who sent into the world Your Beloved Son
    as a light that shines in the darkness,
    invest this wreath, our Advent symbol,
    with the power of Your energy and light.

With each of these candles that is lighted,
    may we rekindle within ourselves the desire
    to prepare a way for the birth of Christ.
With each new candle that is lighted,
    may the flame of Christ's coming
    grow brighter and brighter
    so that this Christmas may see
    a fresh and ever-green coming of the Lord of Light
    into each of our hearts
    and into our whole world.

candle is lit

We pray, then, that the richness of God's blessing
    rest upon this Advent wreath,
    upon our home and upon each of us
    as we light this candle
    in the name of the Father,
    and of the Son
    and of the Holy Spirit.

Amen†

ST. NICHOLAS BLESSING PRAYER
(DECEMBER 6)

St. Nicholas, holy patron of children,
> Bishop of the East,
> we invite you to come among us
> and to grant us your holy blessing.

Help us in this busy, busy season
> not to miss the miracle of the coming of Emmanuel
> in the days of preparation
> as well as on the feast itself.

Help us not to be blind
> to the gifts of getting ready.

Protect us from insincerity.
May every greeting we send
> be signed with love, friendship and prayer.
May our greetings, so written,
> be fun to open and treasures to keep.

Kind St. Nicholas,
> protect us from shopper's fatigue.
Show us how to take delight in the marketplace,
> now transformed in beauty, lights and music.
Save us all from anxiety over what to give
> so that we may concentrate on *how* to give.

Stand by the stepladder
> as we decorate our homes and trees and lives.
May our decorations not be mute
> but rather singing symbols,
> sacred signs of the evergreen coming of the Lord
> of Life.

Help us to remember that mistletoe, holly
and all other ornaments of the season,
were sacred signs to ancient believers.

But, most of all, jolly saint of toys and sweets,
help us stay youthful, humorous, playful and
dream-filled
as we prepare together for the coming of Christ
with Advent longing.

St. Nicholas, pray for us.

Amen✝

BLESSING OF CANDY CANES

Good St. Nicholas, we honor you
    on this your holy feast day.
We rejoice that you are the patron saint
    and the holy symbol of joy
    for many peoples of many lands.
Come, great-hearted saint,
    and be our patron and companion
    as we, once again, prepare our homes and hearts
    for the great feast of Christmas,
    the birth of the Eternal Blessing, Jesus Christ.

May these sweets, these candy canes,
    be a sign of Advent joy for us.
May these candy canes,
    shaped just like your Bishop's staff,
    be for us a sign of your benevolent care.
We rejoice that you are the holy bringer of gifts
    and that so many have been delighted
    through your great generosity.
Help us to be as generous of heart.

Wherever these candy canes are hung,
    on tree or wall or door,
    may they carry with them
    the bright blessing of God.
May all who shall taste them
    experience the joy of God
    upon their tongues and in their hearts.

We ask God, now, to bless
    these your brightly striped sweets
    in the name of the Father,
    and of the Son
    and of the Holy Spirit.

Amen†

BLESSING PRAYER
FOR THE CHRISTMAS TREE

Prayer begins with family gathered around the tree.

Lord of the Forest, Maker of Trees,
    we honor You as we dedicate this tree,
    that it be a sign of Christmas in our home.

Use "symbol of a tree" if tree is artificial.

Green as life are its needled leaves;
    open and inviting are its outstretched branches;
    strong as love is its trunk.

May the blessing of this tree
    call forth from within us
    the memory of our ancient parents
    who worshipped trees as godly.
May we show reverence and care
    toward all the brother and sister trees
    of this our Christmas tree.
May we speak to them and sing them songs,
    enjoy their shade and eat their fruit.
May we learn wisdom from their stories
    and faithfulness from their ever-greenness.

May all trees be for us Christmas trees
    and trees of Life
    as they become incarnations of God
    in our own Garden of Eden.

As Christ died upon the tree of the Cross
　　　that we might be gifted with Life,
　　　may we then remember
　　　that the gifts soon to be placed about this tree
　　　are but reflections of the gifts that came
　　　at the foot of the tree of the Cross.

As sons and daughters of Adam and Eve,
　　　let us rejoice in this tree of Life;
　　　may the spirits of kindness and love
　　　rest upon it.
May the spirit of Christmas
　　　ride in its branches,
　　　this season and for all seasons.

Amen†

A reading from the prophet Isaiah:

The leader or another reads chapter 9, verses 1–2, 5.

Let us pray in silence
    for the coming of peace into the world
    and into our home.

pause for silent prayer

Lord,
    as we pray before this our Christmas crib-shrine
    and await the feast of the Birth of the Holy Child,
    call forth the dormant child from within each of us;
    cause us to wonder and to rejoice again
    in this most ancient feast.

As the magi came bearing gifts,
    may we, this Christmas, gift one another
    with the gold of charity,
    the myrrh of kindness
    and the incense of prayer.

With the shepherds,
    we come to the birth of Christ
    seeking a simple celebration,
    where the greatest gift will be ourselves
    given to You, our God,
    and to each other.

May the star of Bethlehem
    which shone brightly over the first crib

stand guard over our home,
filling it and all the earth
with light and peace.

All present may sing Silent Night *or another Christmas carol.*

We adore You, O Christ, and we bless You
because by Your holy birth
You give hope to all the world.

Amen†

THE FAMILY TABLE
AS
SHRINE
AND
SANCTUARY

One of the most ancient wombs of worship is the family meal. Around this seemingly most common and ordinary of events, has arisen a rich sense of the sacred. To the worshipers of antiquity, life was sacred, and that which nourished life—bread, wine, fruits: all food—was, therefore, holy as well. It was at the meal that the members of the basic unit of society, the family, would remember the great events of the past, remember how God had entered each of their lives and blessed them. Within the simple ritualistic act of eating and drinking, family members celebrated the mysteries of life and remembered protection in difficulties, aid in triumphs and the blessings of good harvests. With feasting, they would rejoice at victories over their enemies; with feasting, they would take joy in the birth of a child; with food, drink, and dancing, they would take pleasure in marriages and the beginning of new families. And at the time of death, they would proclaim a belief in the eternal life of the dead person by once again gathering as a family about the table to partake of food, symbol of life, setting aside portions of that meal for the one who had died.

Out of this ancient tradition, the worship of Israel would find its form. In the Passover Meal, the Children of Israel would remember how the Lord Yahweh had saved them from slavery and led them to freedom. In the festive meals of Sukkoth, Hanukkah, and the other feasts, the family, while at table, would remember the blessings of God and in that remembrance find its faith strengthened.

It was at a dining table and a family feast of the Passover that Jesus would celebrate a most special event with His friends, using the simple foods of bread and wine to make a new and eternal covenant with God. His early followers would gather about such family tables to remember His death and His resurrection and to seal their covenant with one another and with their God.

Thus, the worship and eucharistic celebration of our churches today began at the family table. We need to recall and revive the sacredness of the family meal, to regard eating together as worship and prayer. Once again, we need to view our tables as altar-shrines within the domestic church, the home.

Numerous opportunities are present within our lives for such special and sacred meals: times like birthdays, wedding anniversaries, baptisms, and marriages, as well as great feast days like Christmas, Easter, Thanksgiving and Pentecost. The occasions to feast are as numerous as our imaginations will allow.

From our Jewish traditions, for instance, we can make use of the Sabbath as a weekly occasion for a fine and beautiful meal. It is an event in Jewish homes that is eagerly anticipated by the children and also an occasion for the priestly roles of parents to be externalized. Once a week, on the eve of the Sabbath, the good china and candles are placed on the table. The mother of the family blesses the table and lights the candles with a special prayer. Then the father takes a piece of bread and pronounces a blessing over it; he lifts up a cup of wine and pronounces a blessing over the wine. The bread and the wine, now blessed and dedicated, are passed and shared by all the family. There follows a festive meal which is concluded with a blessing upon the guests and home. By celebrating it on Saturday, the eve of the Christian

Sabbath, this simple meal of love can become a tasty over-ture to the Eucharistic Meal that the family will share with other families at the parish church. A parent or one of the children can read the Sunday Gospel as a means of uniting the family worship with the anticipated parish worship. More important in such a family feast than the words of worship is the sacrament of eating and drinking together. These unspoken symbols are ancient and deeply powerful in bringing the presence of God into our homes and into our lives.

When the family table is seen as an altar-shrine, we will begin to treat it with respect and honor. We should exercise caution that the table and meal times are never forums for discussions of unpleasant subjects or ones that lead to anger. Rather, we should be mindful that the family table is the place where all gather in love and affection; it should be one of the most honored places in the home and stand at the center of the domestic church.

*A plate of bread should be set before the one pronouncing
the blessing. The bread lifted may be a single piece or the
plate of bread itself.*

Lord of the Meal,
    we come to this prayer called grace
    asking that You help us eat this food gracefully
    and with gratitude;
    that we, with grace and care,
    share our lives by word and laughter.
May Your grace, Your life,
    touch us and our food.

    lift up bread

We lift up this bread,
    symbol of life and of Your Son;
    may it and He nourish us this day.

Amen†

Lord, You who gave bread to Moses and his people
    while they traveled in the desert,
    come now, and bless these gifts of food
    which You have given to us.
As this food gives up its life for us,
    may we follow that pattern of self-surrender for
      each other.
May we *be* life to one another.

    lift up bread

With grateful and prayerful hearts,
    we lift up this bread to You.
May Your glory surround it
    and all this meal.

Amen†

A plate of bread should be set before the one pronouncing the blessing. The bread lifted may be a single piece or the plate of bread itself.

Lord God and Giver of All Good Gifts,
    we are grateful as we pause before this meal,
    for all the blessings of life that You give to us.
Daily, we are fed with good things,
    nourished by friendship and care,
    feasted with forgiveness and understanding.
And so, mindful of Your continuous care,
    we pause to be grateful
    for the blessings of this table.

    pause for silent reflection

May Your presence
    be the "extra" taste to this meal
    which we eat in the name of Your Son, Jesus.

Amen✝

Earthmaker and Lord of All Creation,
    we are mindful that this food before us
    has already been blessed by sun, earth and rain.
We pause to be grateful
    for the hidden gifts of life in this food.

    pause for silent reflection

Bless our eyes and taste
    so that we may eat this food
    in a holy and mindful manner.

    lift up bread

We lift up this bread;
    may it be food and symbol
    for all of us who shall eat it.

Amen✝

We have come to the last meal of this day,
    to our supper meal.
Let us be mindful of how our Lord,
    at such a meal as this,
    washed His friends' feet
    in an act of holy service.
As this food is about to serve us as nourishment,
    may we also serve one another.
May the seal of God's love rest upon this food
    and upon this day now drawing to a close.
May we and our gifts of food
    be under the tent of God's peace.

Amen†

The day is coming to a close,
    and, like the disciples on the road to Emmaus,
    we pause to break bread together.
May our eyes be opened,
    and, in this act of common sharing,
    may we see the risen Lord in one another.
May we see the Lord of Life in our food,
    our conversation and lives shared in common.
May the blessing of God,
    His peace and love,
    rest upon our table.

Amen†

A SACRED MEAL RITUAL
FOR THE HOME

Include bracketed sections only if this meal celebration is to be used as a Saturday evening or early Sunday prelude to a communal or parish Eucharist.

The family stands in prayerful silence around their table. Two unlit candles, a plate of bread and a cup of wine or grape juice are on the table. As yet, the food has not been placed on the table but waits, prepared, in the kitchen. After a few moments of silence, the mother of the family begins.

MOTHER: Light is the sacrament
of God's presence among us.
The Lord is our light and our salvation.
We are called to be the children of light,
to be a light unto all nations.
Blessed are You, Lord our God,
who has made us lights to one another.

In the spirit of our ancient traditions,
we now light these festive meal candles.

candles are lit

May our home be made holy, O God, by Your light.
May the light of love and truth shine upon us all
as a blessing from You.
May our table and our family
be consecrated by Your Divine Presence
at this meal and at all our family meals.

Amen†

all are seated in silence

FATHER: (Come, let us welcome
    this first day of a new week: Sunday.
On this day, our Lord Jesus Christ
    did rise from the darkness of the tomb.)
This meal brings blessings to our hearts
    as our workday thoughts and toils are forgotten.
The flames of these holy lights
    shine forth to tell us
    that the spirit of love
    abides within our home.
In that light of love,
    all our good fortunes are seen as blessings,
    and all our griefs and trials are softened.
As we are gathered together at our table,
    God's messenger of peace comes to this table,
    turning the hearts of each of us to one another,
    and deepening the bonds of friendship
    with all those we love.

MOTHER: May we praise You, Lord,
    with this symbol of joy, our family meal.
Thank You, God,
    for the blessings of this past week:
    for life and for love,
    for our health and for friendship
    and for the rewards that have come to us
    from our many labors.

From our ancient traditions
    that flow from their source
    in our holy mother Israel,
    we do now bless these our humble gifts
    of bread and wine.

Father takes a piece of bread, holds it up with his right hand and says:

FATHER: Blessed are You, Lord our God,
> King of the Universe,
> who gives to us bread
> and causes the earth to overflow with good for all.

Father takes a cup of wine, holds it up with his right hand and says:

FATHER: Blessed are You, Lord our God,
> King of the Universe,
> who from the vine
> has created the gift of wine.

May it be for us
> a sign of our love and unity.

First, the blessed bread is passed around the table. Each one breaks off a piece and passes it on to the next person. After the bread has been passed full circle and consumed, then the cup is passed.

When all have finished this ritual, which is done in silence, then the blessing rite continues.

FATHER: Blessed be God and blessed be God's holy name.

ALL TOAST: Happy Feast *or* Happy Sunday!

At this time, the food of the meal is brought to the table. If possible, each member of the family should have some small part in the task of preparing, serving or cleaning up after the meal. The entire meal, from beginning to end, including a festive family cleaning-up and dish drying time, is a time of celebration and enjoyment. When the

meal is finished and before the family leaves the table, the
concluding prayers are said. These prayers could be said by
another member of the family or by a guest.

Prayers following the meal:

FATHER: Let us pause and, in silence,
    be grateful for this meal
    and for the numerous gifts of our home.

pause for silent reflection

Father or another may at this point read a psalm, spoken
prayer or a passage of Sacred Scripture (from this Sunday's
worship).

FATHER: Let us thank our God
    for the Divine presence here at our table.
Blessed be the name of the Lord
    from this time forth and forever.
We bless our God whose food we have eaten
    and who feeds us daily with the bread of goodness.

MOTHER: Blessed be this house and this table;
    blessed be this family
    and all who sit around our table.
Blessed be God
    and blessed be those who live in love.

Amen†

All may together make a sign of the cross.

TABLE BLESSING PRAYER
FOR A WEDDING ANNIVERSARY

Include bracketed section if there are guests present. Two lit candles grace the anniversary table.

ONE: Blessed are You, Lord our God,
    who has united us in holy love.

OTHER: Lord of All History and Divine Keeper of
    Memories,
        we celebrate today the anniversary of our marriage.
We remember that blessed day
        when we were youthful of heart, filled with dreams
        and surrounded by boundless hope
        as we pledged ourselves to one another.
May You, the holy witness to those vows,
        now witness our celebration remembering that day.
We rejoice in the good times—
        in the affection, success, laughter and happiness
        of these years together.
We also embrace the suffering—
        the misunderstandings, injuries and times of separation
        that have been a part of our lives lived together.
These times of darkness
        have been part of our struggling growth
        as two persons who are seeking to be as one.
Like sun and rain,
        joy and sorrow have been mixed together
        to create the rainbow of love
        that has surrounded our marriage.
For all these times and gifts, we are grateful.

ONE: We bless You, Lord of Hearts, in this anniversary
        dinner
      for all that the past years have held for us
      (and for our family).
As the candles burn brightly on our table,
        may the flame of love,
        fed by the mutual loves of our hearts,
        burn brightly before heaven and earth.
We ask Your blessing on this table and this feast.
Bless our marriage, (our children,)
        and all those persons who have helped us grow together.
Lord,
        when another year has passed
        and we come to gather again to celebrate this special day,
        may we find that we have grown in devotion and love
        of each other and of You,
        our God and Divine Matchmaker.
Blessed be this feast
        and the feast of our married life.

Amen✝

Table Liturgy
for the Feast of
Thanksgiving

Included bracketed section if there are guests present.

The family stands in prayerful silence around their table, upon which there are two unlit candles. After a few moments, the mother of the family begins.

MOTHER: Come, let us welcome the feast of
    Thanksgiving
    with joy and with light.
Light is the symbol of the divine.
The Lord is our light and our salvation.
May the light of gratitude burn brightly
    in our hearts
    and around this table,
    not only on the feast of Thanksgiving
    but at all meals.

candles are lit

MOTHER (*or another*): In the silence of our hearts,
    let each of us give thanks
    for all the many gifts that are ours.

pause for silent reflection

Let us also be mindful of those today
    who are without food and a home.

pause for silent reflection

And let us remember those whom we love
    who are not now present at our table.

pause for silent reflection

FATHER: Lord of Gifts,
　　from Your holy heart
　　has come a flood of gifts to us.
With uplifted hearts, we have gathered around this table
　　to thank You with prayer
　　and with the worship of feasting.
We are grateful
　　not only for the gifts of life itself,
　　but for all the gifts
　　of friendship, love, devotion and forgiveness
　　that we have shared.
On this feast of giving thanks, Lord God,
　　we thank You for showing us how to return thanks
　　by lives of service,
　　by deeds of hospitality,
　　by kindness to a stranger
　　and by concern for each other.
(We thank You for the presence of our
　　guests,_____,
　　who, by their being present in our home,
　　have added to the brightness of our celebration.)

We are most grateful, this feast day,
　　for the way You, our hidden God,
　　have become visible to us
　　in one another,
　　in countless daily gifts
　　and in the marvels of creation.
Come, Lord of Gifts,
　　and bless our table and all the food of this feast.

Let us thank the Lord,
　　today and all days. Amen.

ALL TOAST: Happy Thanksgiving!

TABLE LITURGY
FOR THE FEAST OF CHRISTMAS

Include bracketed sections if there are guests present.

The family stands in prayerful silence around their table, upon which there are two unlit candles. After a few moments, the father of the family begins.

166 FATHER: Blessed are You, Lord our God,
      who has gathered us together
      at this our Christmas feasting table.

MOTHER: As we light our candles on this feast of light,
      may the eternal light of God
      that shines with splendor in the stars
      shine upon our table and fill our home.
May the spirit of God
      that shone in the star of Bethlehem
      surround our table
      and fill our food and our hearts with its holy light.

candles are lit

FATHER: Let us, each,
      on this great and holy feast of the birth of our Savior,
      pause now and, in silence,
      lift up our hearts to God in gratitude.

pause for silent prayer

FATHER or MOTHER: Lord of All Gifts,
      our home is filled with joy and great beauty
      on this feast of Christmas.

We each come to this our Christmas feast
   with eagerness and a happy heart.
As a family,
   we thank You for the gifts of food upon this table,
   mindful that You, our God,
   make every day of the year a Christmas
   where we are gifted by You.
We thank You that we are together
   to share the happiness of this ancient holy day.
(We thank You for the presence of our
   guests,_____,
   who, by their being present in our home,
   have added to the brightness of our celebration.)

FATHER *or* MOTHER: Lord of All Gifts,
   Holy Father of our Savior Jesus,
   with fullness of heart
   we now ask Your holy blessing upon our food,
   and upon our family
   (and our honored guests
   who have joined us for this great feast).
May Your blessing be upon us all,
   in the name of the Father,
   and of the Son and of the Holy Spirit. Amen.

ALL TOAST: Merry Christmas *or* A Blessed Christmas!

TABLE LITURGY
FOR THE FEAST OF
EASTER SUNDAY

Include bracketed section if there are guests present.

The family stands in prayerful silence around their table,
upon which there are two unlit candles. After a few
moments, the father of the family begins.

FATHER: Blessed are You, Lord our God,
who raised up Jesus from the tomb
and has gathered all of us around this table.

MOTHER: As the light of God
overcame the darkness of death,
may these candles we now light
be for us a sign of the flame of life
that burns within our hearts.

candles are lit

As these Easter candles
call us to the feast of this our table,
may the light of Christ,
call us to Your eternal Easter feast.
May these candles delight our eyes
and add splendor to our meal.

FATHER: With great joy,
we come to our Easter dinner
as we continue our celebration

of the ever-newness of the resurrection
of our Lord and Savior, Jesus Christ.
We rejoice in the resurrection of spring,
as birds, flowers and fields come alive
after the long sleep of winter.
May we, in this Easter Sunday meal,
share with them the great joy of life.
Let us pause and, in silence,
lift up our hearts to God
in gratitude for this holy Easter meal.

pause for silent prayer

(As our Risen Lord came as a guest
and ate with His disciples,
may we be grateful for the presence at our table
of our guests, _____,
who bring to our table the holy presence of God
and add to our celebration of this great and joyful
feast.
May God bless them,
for together with the food of this feast,
they give us reason for joy.)

MOTHER: May the taste of goodness in this food
be a promise of the eternal Easter meal
we shall all share together with our Risen Lord.
May this Easter dinner be a sacrament
of springtime, peace and eternal happiness.
Alleluia, Alleluia!
May God's blessing rest upon this table
and each of us. Amen.

ALL TOAST: Happy Easter *or* A Blessed Easter!

THANKSGIVING TABLE PRAYER (BRIEF FORM)

Lord God,
>   our hearts are crowded with gratitude
>   as we celebrate the feast of Thanksgiving.
We have come to this our feasting table
>   with great joy and eagerness,
>   for we are truly grateful to You, our God,
>   for all that we have been given.
We pause now and, in silent prayer,
>   do thank You for the great generosity of Your gifts.

>   *pause for silent reflection*

We also thank one another for gifts—
>   especially for the gifts of love and affection
>   that we have freely shared.
We are thankful
>   for all who are present at this our feast
>   (*names of guests may be mentioned*)
>   as well as for all those who have labored in love
>   in order to bring this dinner to our table.

May You, our God, bless this Thanksgiving feast
>   and all of us who shall share it
>   in Your holy name: Father, Son and Holy Spirit.

Amen†

CHRISTMAS DAY
TABLE PRAYER
(BRIEF FORM)

Lord God of Life,
>together with the beautiful traditions
>of decorating the Christmas tree,
>of singing carols and giving gifts,
>this Christmas dinner is an important part
>of our celebration of the birth
>of our Lord, Jesus Christ.

Come, Lord our God,
>and surround our feast day table
>as we delight in this joyous season of Christmas.

Gift us in this meal with the taste of happiness
>as we savor this coming together
>of family and friends.

As sparkling stars and singing angels rejoiced
>at the birth of the Christ Child in Bethlehem,
>so may we take great joy
>in this our Christmas dinner-celebration.

May You, our God, bless it and us
>in Your holy name: Father, Son and Holy Spirit.

Amen†

PRAYER FOR BLESSING TRADITIONAL EASTER FOODS: BREAD, SALT, AND EGGS

The blessed food is intended to be the first eaten at the Easter breakfast. As such the blessing traditionally takes place on Holy Saturday afternoon or upon returning home from the resurrection worship service.

Lord, Supreme Spirit of All Creation,
>   as we rejoice
>   in the resurrection of our Lord, Jesus Christ,
>   we place before You
>   these gifts of Easter food.
From our own ancient traditions,
>   we have prepared these three ageless signs of life:
>   bread, salt, and eggs,
>   and we ask that You now bless them.

Fill these simple gifts with secret energy,
>   with healing and mystical power:
>   bread to nourish our life,
>   salt to preserve the hope of Easter morning
>   and the egg, the eternal sign
>   of the divine life hidden in each of us.

May these three blessed gifts of food
>   grace all who shall eat them.
May the family table where they are shared
>   be illuminated with the light
>   of our Easter feast day celebration.

May our table be richly blessed
   with the holiness, joy, and peace
   of Your Easter altar table.

May the ageless blessing of Your divine name,
   Father, Son, and Holy Spirit,
   be upon these Easter gifts of new life.

Amen✝

EASTER SUNDAY TABLE PRAYER (BRIEF FORM)

Creative God and Lord of Life,
> You who call forth from the darkness of death
> all those who love You,
> we rejoice, on this Easter Sunday,
> in the resurrection from the dead
> of our Lord, Jesus Christ.

174 Visit our home and this table
> with Your bright blessing of peace and life.

❖ We pause in the midst of this prayer
> to remember all the holy dead of our family
❖ > who live now in You and who await
> the final and glorious resurrection of the dead.

❖
pause for silent reflection

❖ May they and we,
> because of our faith in You, our God,
❖ > taste in the victory of life over death.
May the Risen Christ, our Lord and Savior,
❖ > be our guest as we celebrate His resurrection
> with this Easter Sunday dinner.
Bless those whose work to prepare this meal
> has truly been a work of prayer,
> and bless all of us who shall share it
> with Easter love and joy.

May You, then, bless this table and this food,
> and each of us
> in Your holy name: Father, Son, and Holy Spirit.

Amen†

SHRINES
IN
THE
DOMESTIC
CHURCH

Religious images that are icons are valuable aids to prayer and, in their very essence, are prayers. Icons are not merely pictures intended to decorate the walls of our homes but are doorways to the sacred. A crucifix, statue or holy image, as such, is a sacred center for prayer which lifts up our hearts and minds—through the hearts of the saints or the Sacred Heart of Christ—to the Divine Mystery that resides within.

Because of their nature, we should be mindful in how we handle—with our bodies and our minds—these sacred icons. Religious images should be prayerfully placed on the wall at those times, for example, when we move into a new home or upon newly acquiring a holy icon. Further, when cleaning or moving demand that we take down our crucifix or Madonna, it should be done with a prayer. Always, we should have a consciousness that the pictured image itself holds a key to the mystery that is contained within it. Such an awareness will call forth reverence from those who own a sacred image.

A number of safeguards can be employed to help insure that this attitude of reverence be sustained. Too many images tend to defuse their purpose; one or two well chosen and well placed icons are of more value than a multitude. Further, if we form the habit of praying before these sacred doorways which we call images, we will prevent the habit of seeing them and yet not seeing them from taking root. How often do the pictures or photos that we have in our homes blend into the woodwork and become unseen! In response to this tendency toward habit-blindness, the ancient Chinese took up the custom of changing their pictures every few months. With the sacred images of our home, borrowing from this wise practice may be beneficial. Slight variations with the different seasons of the year—at Christmas, Lent, Easter, Pentecost, as well as on special saint days like those of Patrick or Nicholas—can provide freshness in our religious remembering and devotion. A fresh attitude is also necessary for seasonal religious images like the Christmas tree or crib. They are not intended to be mere resting spots for Christmas toys but holy and sacred doorways to prayer. We need to rescue them from the realm of mere decorations and restore to them their original holy purpose.

When does an image of a religious nature become a sacred icon? That which is beautiful, honest and true will always be holy, but often that which is sold as holy is far from possessing an artistic beauty. Yet, even a holy card or a picture from a religious calendar—the simplest of images— can become sacred if we use it with prayer, devotion and faith. What is important in the beauty of an icon lies beyond the rules of color, line and artistic form. And what is really important is how we treat the image.

Few are the domestic churches that possess a real treasure of sacred art. Such a treasure need not be a painting by Michelangelo or Raphael but is more likely to be a religious image that has been handed down from generation to generation—a cross or a painting of the Mother of God, for example, that has absorbed years and years of prayers. We who are citizens of the age of technology easily forget the power that is present in a rosary that was owned and cherished by a grandparent or a prayerbook that belonged to one of our parents. Such sacred relics of the domestic church radiate power and grace. When we feel unable to pray, when words of praise are absent, these family sacred treasures can be invaluable aids; we should simply sit in their presence allowing their holiness to seep out into our troubled lives.

Young families that wish to begin traditions would do well to search for a beautiful crucifix or an icon of Christ or His Blessed Mother that would be worthy of being passed on to one's children's children. But there is a cost involved in coming upon such a religious heirloom. We think nothing of spending hundreds of dollars for a television set that will last perhaps five to ten years, while some cheap plastic image is often selected to adorn the shrine of our home. The issue is not so much one of money but, rather, of the type of material used for the icon and the quality of its workman- ship. The most important ingredient is the care and love that goes into selecting or creating it. A real treasure would be a sacred piece of art that was carved by a member of the family, painted by someone in the domestic church itself. A simple wooden cross made by the father of the family will become more precious than a great masterpiece as it day to day soaks up the prayers of parents, children and all who revere it.

An icon is an image that aids our imagination and supports our prayer to an invisible God. As a symbol, it radiates what is beyond word and image and calls our hearts to the mysterious presence of the Divine Mystery. We need not restrict ourselves to handmade images, for God has left His fingerprints, His image, in all of creation. The golden leaf of an oak, the empty nest of birds, a rock from a special place we have visited—these and innumerable other works of creation can become our holy images. We need never fear for the quality of their workmanship: each of them is a masterpiece from the art museum called creation. As well as being fine art, each of these natural icons is also filled with grace and wonder, inviting us to find holiness in all that is natural.

Finally, we must always remember that God is spirit and, as Jesus told us, must be worshipped in spirit and in truth. We must always acknowledge that the holiness of icons in the domestic church rests not in the paintings or crucifixes, but in the people who live there! We are each images of God, before whom, if we fully understood that mystery, we would bow and pause in the greatest of reverence. May the holy images of our home call forth from us profound reverence for each other as doorways to the sacred mystery of God.

BLESSING PRAYER
AND DEDICATION FOR A
SACRED IMAGE IN THE HOME

Lord God, Divine Artist of All That is Beautiful,
    we ask that Your holy blessing
    rest upon this image (of_____)
    that we are now placing within our home.

Image is reverently set in its special place.

We pause in silent prayer to look upon this sacred image
    and to call upon You, our God,
      to bless us with Your Holy Presence as we do so.

    pause for silent prayer

May this sacred image
    be for us a sign of You, our Invisible God,
    a sign for Your continuous presence here within our
      home.
May this image (of_____)
    be for us who live here
    a doorway to Your Divine Heart.

May it be for us
    a gathering place for prayer
    in times of sorrow and trial,
    in times of great rejoicing and blessing.
Help each of us to treat it with reverence and respect.
Help us not to become so dulled by the familiarity of
      time
    that our eyes fail to see its meaning and purpose
    in our home.

May this sacred image protect our home
   from evil, from the danger of storm,
      from the terror of war and the bitterness of anger
         and hate.
May all who look upon this sacred image
   be blessed by You, our God.
With reverence, we acknowledge its place of honor
   among us
      that it may give You glory and honor
      and be for us a blessing.

Amen✝

Each person present may kiss the image.

A Single Person's Blessing Prayer for a Sacred Image

Lord God of Heaven and Earth,
    all creation is filled with holy images of You—
    trees, flowers, rivers, and hills
    and all Your living creatures—
    and each speaks unceasingly
    of Your beauty and love.
May this sacred symbol
    which I now prepare to bless
    be for me a daily reminder of You,
    my Lord and Beloved One.
May this image be a source of grace and power
    in times of joy
    and in times of sorrow as well.

Mindful of the power of Your divine blessing,
    I now dedicate this image
    in praise of Your name:
    Father, Son, and Holy Spirit.

Amen✝

BLESSING PRAYER FOR THE SACRED IMAGE OF A SAINT

Lord God, holy are You.
Your saints and holy ones perpetually give You glory,
    and, in their holiness as well as their humanness,
    they are channels of Your grace for us.
May this holy image of _(name of saint)_
    be for all of us who shall look upon it,
    who shall touch it and pray before it,
    a source of Your rich blessings
    and a gateway to Your loving Presence.
May the good example
    and the special virtues that _(name of saint)_ embodied
    be a holy pattern for our daily lives.
May the grace and help
    of all the Communion of Saints be with us
    as we journey homeward to You,
    the Eternal Source of All Holiness.
Bless this image, Lord and God,
    in Your holy name.

Amen✝

Blessing Prayer
for a Sacred Image
of the Mother of God

Come, God of Heaven and Earth,
    and be present with us
    as we bless this image of Mary,
    the Mother of our Lord, Jesus Christ.
By placing this image of the Blessed Mother
    here as a shrine in our home,
    we hope for her special intercession
    before You and all the court of heaven.
May the honor we give to this image of Mary
    increase our love for You, our God,
    and for her Son, Jesus Christ.

May Your power and healing, Almighty God,
    fill all the space that this image looks out on,
    keeping away all evil and danger.
May she, who took to heart
    the predicament of a young couple
    and asked Jesus to perform His first miracle
    of changing water into wine,
    be an intercessor to her divine Son
    for our daily needs as well.

Grant, Eternal Source of All That Is,
    that we who pray to You before this icon of Mary
    may daily grow in holiness
    as we give honor to her.

May the divine blessing of Your name,
    Father, Son and Holy Spirit,
    be upon this sacred image now and forever.

Amen✝

*The Hail Mary may be recited by all taking part: each may
then in turn come and kiss the sacred image.*

DEVOTIONS
TO
THE
MOTHER
OF
GOD

Devotion to the Mother of God, Mary, in both public and private worship, is one of the most ancient prayers of the faithful. This devotion has found various expressions. Numerous forms of prayer, pilgrimages to her shrines, veneration of her icons and the keeping of great feast days are among the many displays of honor and love. As the mother of our Lord, she has been accounted great honor and affection through the years. Recently, though, our attention has been focused on other areas of prayer, and we are beginning to experience an absence of devotion to the Blessed Mother.

Within our religious tradition are found numerous beautiful prayers, songs and liturgical services honoring the Mother of God. Hymns such as *O Maria* and prayers such as the *Hail Mary* and the *Hail Holy Queen* have been a source of inspiration to the faithful over the centuries. By their frequent and devout use, these and other ancient prayers have become storehouses of grace.

The rosary has been and still remains at the center of Marian devotional prayers. It is an incarnational prayer; body and heart pray in harmony as the fingers move along the chain of communion with God and the Blessed Mother. To simply hold the rosary in one's hands without saying any words is to be in prayer. This is especially true if the rosary we hold has belonged to our own mother or father, to a grandparent or other ancestor. Such a family rosary has been blessed by years of devotion and has been a relic, holy and grace-full. In times of trouble or times of great joy, while traveling or when sick, these holy prayer beads allow our hearts to be collected, calmed and Christ-filled in this ancient prayer of praise.

We are not limited only to these expressions of devotion and should not fear to form new devotions and prayers that will express our love for the Mother of God, in this age and in this part of the world. Especially, devotions to Mary as Mother and Holy Wife, Prophetic Woman, Priestly Lady and Bride of the Spirit are called for in our times. Perhaps, we can also celebrate new Marian festivals that will inspire us in these first years of the twenty-first century.

Feast days of the Mother of God offer numerous opportunities for family prayer and for celebrations within the home. These celebrations within the domestic church, the home, can allow us to be mindful of the different ways in which we have need of the prayerful intercession of Mary, the Blessed Mother. Each feast of hers is also an occasion for us to remember in prayer our own mothers, whether living or dead, and the beautiful gifts of prayer, grace and love we have received from them. Each feast of Mary gives the further opportunity of praying in union with our common mother, the earth. As we honor and respect the Mother of God, we can reflect on and strive to show reverence toward the earth, water, air and all creation. At these times, we also have occasion to sing the praises of those noble and holy women who have labored over the centuries to usher in the kingdom of God. Mary of Nazareth, who carried the Word of God within her body, became the Gospel Woman. And such, she is a royal lady who leads the procession of those saints who lived in the spirit of the Gospel. Whenever we gather for prayers or table meals in honor of Mary, the Womb of God, we are presented with a challenge to wholeness. Each of us, woman or man, has the opportunity to reaffirm that which is feminine within us, that which is gentle, compassionate, warm and loving, darkly creative, fertile and willing to surrender to the divine will. Each special day honoring Mary can challenge us to unfold these qualities in our prayers and in our lives. The Church—and every person who seeks perfection and wholeness—needs such a devotion to the Woman of God, Mary.

The Church has traditionally, on these special days, commemorated the blessed motherhood of Mary in the most effective of all teachings: feasting! Her festivals are among the most charming and beautiful, and it is a shame that we no longer celebrate by parading and dancing in the streets as Christians once did on such feasts. We can, however, celebrate with feasting in our homes. When these feast days come, we can find simple and suitable ways to adorn our picture or shrine of the Mother of God. A vigil light, candle or flowers (perhaps daisies or marigolds) can be placed before her image or upon our meal table. We can also make a special shrine around a statue as was the custom with the use of a May altar to honor Mary. And we may crown these festive touches in the joyous celebration of a family meal.

Each season has its own Marian feast which we can rediscover and rejuvenate according to our culture and our times. March 25, the feast of the Annunciation, can also become a festival in honor of the coming of spring, the awakening of our mother earth to the fruitfulness of life as Mary became awakened to Divine Life on that day. The feast of the Assumption of Mary on August 15 is a wonderful time in our part of the world for a harvest festival. This feast honors the completion, the harvest, of her life, and it is fitting to use the fruits of the land in aiding us to celebrate such a feast. In the autumn of the year, on October 7, we keep the feast of the Holy Rosary. As autumn in all her glory portrays the sunset of life, we can at this time honor Mary, not as a young virgin but as mother, as matriarch of the early Church. Like autumn, she grew old graced with wisdom and holy beauty. We can honor her as the elderly Queen of the Apostles, Ark of Holy Tradition and Living Anchor of Faith. Such a feast reminds us of the reverence we should show to all those in the autumn of life. In December, we celebrate two great feast days, the Immaculate Conception on December 8 and the feast of Our Lady of Guadalupe on December 12. We may choose either of these to reflect on the open womb of the Virgin awaiting the coming of Emmanuel. Such a winter feast of Mary can be an important part of our prayerful preparation for Christmas.

These four seasonal feasts and the other feast days of Mary during the Church year can offer times for family prayer and for feasting, which have always been a part of the Christian celebration. By private prayer, by pilgrimage, and family prayer at the table, these feasts of the Mother of God can allow us to experience a great treasury of beauty, tradition and blessings. Those who with devotion and love honor the Blessed Mother are blessed in return by God.

Holy Mary,
>Mother of our Lord Jesus Christ,
>priestly woman and holy prophetess,
>who carried in your very body
>the Gospel of Peace—
>we greet you,
>and we ask you to be our mother as well.

188   Holy Mother of God,
>whose sign in our presence is creation,
>whose sacrament is the earth,
>mother who is to us both womb and tomb—
>we praise you.

Your jewels are the riches of beauty in all creation
>sparkling forth in flower bloom,
>bird wing, and rainbow-singing-sign.

We honor you, Mary, wife of Joseph and mother of Christ.

Hostess to angels, patroness to contemplatives,
>guide to pilgrims, inspiration to poets,
>light to those who wander in the darkness
>in response to the voice of God—
>we honor you
>and ask to be united with you.

United with you, we will be one with God.
United with you, we will be open to the will of God.
United with you, we too will feel the mystery of Christ,
>alive within us.

Holy Mary, Mother of God,
>pray for us.

Amen†

Prayer
to the Mother of God in Gratitude for Gifts Received

Honor be yours,
    O Mother of God.
We rejoice in thanksgiving
    for signs of God's love.
We take great joy in the fruitfulness of the earth,
    in good harvests, in full barns
    and in the special signs given to us this day.

We are grateful for the harvest-fullness
    of life itself,
    for the blessings of health
    and the fruits of the Spirit which have come to us.

Together with all those who love your Son, Jesus,
    we rejoice in Him
    who was the fruit of your womb,
    the harvest gift of history
    and an eternal blessing to each of us.

Mary,
    Blessed Mother and gateway to mystic love,
    help us to be united with all those
    who love God and seek truth.
May our gratitude this day
    for the special gifts that have come to us,
    be praise and honor
    for our God, the Lord of All Gifts.

Holy Mary, Mother of God,
    we thank you for your intercession
    and ask that you carry our prayer of gratitude
    straightaway to the heart of God.

Amen†

Holy Mary, Mother of our Lord,
>with confidence and trust,
>I come to you and ask your holy intercession,
>for I am in need.

I am more than mindful
>of the numerous gifts and blessings that are mine.
Indeed, my life is overflowing
>with signs of God's eternal love.
This day, however, finds me in special need,
>and so I come before you,
>O Holy Mother.

I place into your supple hands
>my special need this day (of_____).

Holy Mother,
>I am aware that God knows my every need
>and does not have to be reminded of my necessities.
At the same time, I am mindful
>of your great compassion
>and know the grace
>of your being with me in prayer,
>and so I lay this special intention before you
>with great confidence.

Reminded of your Son,
>who often came to you with His needs,
>I am at ease

as I follow in His steps
and bring my needs before you.

In asking this favor of our God,
I follow your holy example
and bow before the divine will,
willingly embracing
what God has chosen for me.

Amen†

Mary, Holy Mother of God,
>   we salute you and we honor you.

In this season of darkness,
>   as we await the coming feast
>   of the birth of the Son of God,
>   we do pray to you, mother of the Lord of Light.
Hail to you,
>   Holy Sun Virgin, Our Lady of Guadalupe,
>   Patroness of the Americas.

We watch the winter sun,
>   our source of heat and light, our calendar maker,
>   as it wanes
>   and prepares for rebirth.
Holy sun, mystic mother of ages past,
>   be for us a living sign.

Holy Virgin of Tepayac, with the sun as your mantel,
>   you who are clothed in yellow light,
>   with the moon under your feet
>   and stars for your crown,
>   we honor you.
Holy earth mother, holy lady of the star-filled night,
>   mother of candles and lamps,
>   we praise you.

We thank you for the protection of our land,
    for your loving kindness and many gifts.
Protect our home, guard our family
    and watch over us forever.

We ask this of you through the mystery of your Son,
    who lives with the Father and the Holy Spirit,
    and all those who have gone before us,
    forever and ever.

Amen†

A
Hermitage
in
Every
Home

We know from the Gospels that Jesus frequently withdrew from His daily life to spend time in prayer and solitude. This is a truly human need, for silence and solitude are necessary for all of us who desire to grow in holiness. Without quiet leisure, the springs of life soon dry up; and so, if we desire that our homes and our lives be creatively happy, we, like our Lord, must find the time and the space for solitude. While Jesus lived near the mountains and could easily slip away for time alone, most of us do not and, therefore, must find our own individual, creative ways to meet this need.

A hermitage is a special type of house, a house of silence and solitude. It can be a single room or composed of many, but what is important is that it be furnished with stillness and the space to reflect, study or simply be alone. In ancient Russia, every village, it is said, had its hermitage or poustinia. But our city or neighborhood may lack such a religious sanctuary. This need not deter us, for every home has the marvelous possibility of containing this specially created "holy space." We might find a place for our hermitage in a den, a bedroom or even in the basement; it might be any place in the home that, through common agreement among members of the family, no one will disturb during its time as a hermitage.

If we have decided to spend a day or an afternoon in prayer, it will be of value to prepare for our home-hermitage experience. We can start to set apart its time and space by selecting a beginning blessing prayer. We should next determine the length of time we want to spend apart. If we intend to have a full day of solitude, we need to consider the role of food. It is important that our time be free of all household duties and routines, and not eating is a possible way of allowing this freedom. As an alternative to a total fast, some simple food such as a bit of bread or tea may be taken so that we do not spend our time thinking about how hungry we are. Similarly, the place we choose should be comfortable; if it is too hot or too cold, our bodies will be talking to us so loudly that we will never hear the voice of God. Next, we should choose what we want to take with us into this sacred and special space. Scripture or other spiritual reading, with perhaps some simple creative activity like drawing or sewing, may be helpful in initiating our first attempts at being alone and doing . . . nothing! Whatever allows us to be comfortable, at ease and able to enjoy this time apart is good. We should begin where we are and not rush into that which is beyond us. Begin slowly, and allow a taste for solitude to grow with each time this type of prayer is taken up. As we come to savor this prayer of solitude, we should try to set aside a hermitage day, or poustinia day, at least once a month. The name we decide to call it is not of prime concern; what is important—very important to our spiritual growth—is that we actually do spend time alone in stillness.

A few simple rules for how to proceed with the prayer of the hermitage can help make our time more fruitful. Rule number one is to be simple—simple in our desires and expectations. God comes to us in simple ways, and so, we do not seek the spectacular—we seek only stillness, that unique healing for body and soul. Rule number two: we must be patient as we attempt to quiet the mind and body. Our modern lives are so supercharged with noise and activity that all parts of our persons echo this tension. We will be tempted to leave a prayer of solitude for more "productive" work; yet, if we can be patient and let the mind and body relax, we will find that being apart and being still *produces* great things in our lives!

Rule three involves a recognition that we are not alone when we are by ourselves. We should be aware that we are one with those whom we love, with the members of our family and with all the Church. In addition, a powerful means of grace is available in consciously uniting ourselves

with others who are sitting in stillness. Across this earth, a great many people contribute to an unceasing prayer of solitude: hermits and contemplatives in monasteries, caves and hermitages, as well as countless other busy people like ourselves who have set aside a time and place for quiet prayer and reflection. Daily, a network of light and grace radiates among those who sit outside of the rush and roar of life to be absorbed in the Divine Mystery. We should unite ourselves with them, allowing a communion of grace and prayer to support us when we get anxious and want to leave our temporary hermitage.

The prayer of solitude should be part of a pattern of prayer in our lives so that it can nourish us on a regular basis. But there will be times outside this pattern when we may have to announce to the family that the bedroom or den will become a hermitage for the next hour or so. These may be times of choice and decision, times of sorrow and pain, or times of misunderstanding. In these circumstances, we need space and prayer so that we can properly allow what has happened to be a means of growth in love instead of a cause for tearing apart the fabric of the family. These special times when we feel the need to be alone are times when we seek the hermitage of the heart. The formation of this hidden hermitage will require a real physical place so that our hearts can be shaped by the experience of solitude and stillness. Ultimately, after much practice, we will be able to find solitude and silence wherever we are.

There still remains the sticky question of how to maintain the home-hermitage as a place of quiet within an often hectic household. We should not be ashamed to discuss our needs, especially our spiritual needs, with the members of our family. Even small children, and perhaps they more than the more adult members of the family, can understand that this "space" is special, indeed, sacred. In their games, they are continuously creating magical and special places with the simplest of means. Those who create a hermitage within the home are creating magic space and so become the sort of children for whom Jesus said the gates of the kingdom would swing open. The rest of the family should understand that this room, at this time, is special. The usual noise of the home is to be suspended for the "special" hours. Demands are not to be made upon parents while they are "in the hermitage." If this prayer takes place when both parents are at home, one can take over the duties of answering the phone or door so that the other can be free. Parents may at first be hesitant to ask children not to play radios or to talk to them during these special times, yet the very discipline necessary becomes an outward sign of the necessity of prayer. Children learn how to pray not just by parents teaching them prayers but more so by the example of parents who pray. Even youngsters can be invited to have their hermitage or hide-out where they are free to go after being punished or when life is bitter for them, as well as for short times when they simply wish to be left alone. If we but think about it, being alone and finding that experience joyful is really to return to being a child. The child within us, even if we are in our eighties, delights in the opportunity to meet the Mystery within and to take playful delight in a special, sacred and magical world.

BLESSING PRAYER FOR A PLACE TO BE USED AS A HERMITAGE

My Lord and my God,
> You did call, from their busy daily lives,
> Your servants Moses, Elijah, John the Baptist,
> Mary of Nazareth and Your Son, Jesus,
> to come apart and to spend time in solitude.

Some You have called to the desert,
> some to mountain peaks,
> others to the hidden hermitage within their homes.

I have heard that ancient desert call
> and seek to be alone with You.

Since I lack a nearby mountain or desert,
> I will use this space that I have.

My Lord, You who are the creator of all space,
> You who make lonely desert places holy,
> come and consecrate this place
> as a temporary hermitage for me.

Cleanse it of noise
> and anything that might call me out of its stillness.

May this space, sacred by Your blessing,
> become for me a waiting room
> where I shall wait upon You,
> my Lord, my Beloved, my Friend.

May prayerful peace flow outward from here,
> touching with grace all those whom I love
> and all the earth as well.

May all dark powers be impotent,
    unable to cross the sacred circle
    that surrounds this holy hermitage.
Help me, my Lord, to leave outside this hermitage
    my plans for tomorrow, my memories of yesterday,
    as I live fully and completely
    in the wonder of Your present moment.

Lord, may my prayer be one with that of all persons
    who throughout this earth are in solitude and
    stillness, forming a luminous and silent hymn
      of glory to You.

May Your blessing, Almighty God,
    Father, Son, and Holy Spirit,
    be upon this hermitage and this solitary time.

Amen†

PRAYER
BEFORE LEAVING
A HERMITAGE OR ENDING
A TIME OF SOLITUDE

My Lord, it is time for me to return.
I thank You for this quiet time apart,
        unburdened by my normal duties of life.
This time alone
        has been renewing and re-creating for me
        as body and spirit have been healed.
Its rest has given a boost to my body.
Its silence has been as a salve to my spirit.
This time apart from others
        has renewed within me a desire to be in communion
        with all those whom I love.
Fire within me the desire
        to join them and all others
        on the crowded journey of life.

I thank You, O Secret One,
        for the graces of this time in solitude.
Each time I withdraw to be alone,
        I learn more not to fear being alone.
I thus prepare myself for that final moment
        when I shall pass through the desert of death,
        with its absolute aloneness,
        and come to absolute communion of life eternal
        with You.

My Lord, I treasure this time now ending.
Help me, as I return to the flow of daily life.
Prepare me for what I shall find,
    the good and the bad,
    mistakes and successes—
    whatever You have laid out for me.

May this holy time of prayerful solitude
    fill me with the necessary energy
    to once again take up the challenge
    of finding holiness in the midst of my work,
    in the center of my home.

Come, my Beloved,
    and accompany me as I return
    to the crowded and noisy crossroads of life.

Amen†

DAILY
PERSONAL
PRAYERS

In all the great religious traditions of the world, an important place is given to private or personal prayer. This prayer may take various forms but usually involves some type of daily discipline. These daily prayer times are an individual's expression of a personal relationship with God. As such, they are times of devotion, gratitude, personal piety and occasions for petitions for personal needs. Universally, the sacred times are sunrise and sunset; it is in the morning and evening that persons have traditionally sought a communion with the mystery of God that dwells within.

These times of private prayer need not be long, and it is often better that they be brief. Private prayer should be measured by quality and not quantity. Ideally, some of this time should be reserved for silent prayer or meditation. We can begin with five to ten minutes of silence and with practice increase this period to fifteen or twenty minutes. For some, it may not be feasible to pray twice a day. For these, a morning period might be preferred, since late at night we are often too tired physically and emotionally to pray. Just as we do not begin our day without taking proper time to wash ourselves and groom our hair, so we should take time to properly care for the needs of the inner-person and to acknowledge our position as creatures before an almighty and loving God. If we are unable to set aside a block of time for private prayer, we should at least attempt to begin and to conclude our day with a brief act of prayerful union with God. No one's day is too busy for at least that minimum expression of personal prayer!

We should come to daily prayer fully aware that we are a blend, a beautiful blend, of body, mind and spirit. These sacred three must each enter into the time of prayer aware of the needs of the others. While it is possible to pray anywhere, in an easy chair or on our knees, for those who understand the unity of body and spirit, the position of the body while at prayer is important. Our chosen position of prayer may be kneeling, sitting in a yoga posture, or sitting upright in a straight-back chair. What is important in whatever position we take up is that it permits us to stay alert, frees the body from stress and also allows the body to pray nonverbal prayers. Such prayers without words can be sacred actions such as a profound bow, perhaps touching the head to the floor, in an act of adoration and surrender to the will of God. The prayer of the body may include the use of our hands, eyes, ears or feet as instruments of devotion. Coming from within the Western tradition of thought, formed as it is by Greek thinking, we may find it difficult to consider prayer as an expression of the whole person and not simply as an exercise of the mind. The mind is but part of the total person, and it is the whole person that should come to the time of prayer. The more of the whole person that prays—mind, heart, imagination, memory, senses, as well as dreams, disappointments, sorrows and joys—the more wholesome and holy will be our prayer.

The old rabbis said that a person who has been on a journey should not pray until three days after returning! They understood the inclination of the inner-person to absorb the surrounding environment—the noise and the confusion of the road—and the need to let this inner noise melt away. Considering the noise and stress of our modern lives, we can understand why it is difficult for people to pray. Aware of our capacity to absorb all the happenings around us, we should take time to cleanse the inner-person of all tension, noise and stress. Each time of prayer should begin with the prayer of quieting. During this time, we strive to prayerfully quiet the body, the mind and the spirit and to bring them into a calm harmony. By a gentle slowing down, we can "scrub" our hearts of anything that may block the flow of our prayer. As doctors scrub before an operation, we can cleanse ourselves of anything that makes our heart unfit for a time of communion with God. With gentleness, we should breathe out the trials and troubles that press in upon us. When we are at peace, then we can begin our formal prayer.

As far as it is possible, it is of value to pray at the same hour each day and in the same place within our home. These two seemingly small details can provide great assistance in developing a daily discipline of prayer. A pattern of prayer that allows us familiar surroundings at a certain time of day helps to surround the heart with support when we come to our private devotion. A regular routine makes it easier to quiet ourselves, easier to enter into prayer. We can choose such places as a corner of a bedroom, a spot in front of a sacred image or a space before a window that opens onto the rising sun. We may also wish to use incense, a lit candle or a small altar to create an atmosphere that will support and give expression to our time of prayer. Again, if for some reason we must bypass prayer, at one of our regular times, we can at least reinforce our prayer-discipline by pausing briefly before a sacred image of Christ or His Blessed Mother. In that brief moment, we can dedicate our day to the honor and glory of God. A profound bow or a sign of the cross before this room-shrine can spiritually energize us for the day's work that is about to begin.

The prayer forms for each day of the week that follow are intended to provide a beginning point for your daily prayers of devotion. Though they are arranged for morning and evening, as your personal prayer pattern develops, you may find it necessary to reshape the text to fit your chosen time of day. Each form has allowed for a time when you may pray a psalm or one of the prayers found in this handbook, such as a blessing prayer or a prayer to the Mother of God. However, the forms are intended to be a guide and should, therefore, be flexible. Each person should feel free to shape, re-form and arrange these prayers so that they will be expressions of devotion that are from the very heart.

Individual prayer should be just that: individual and personal. All true prayer leads us always to the heart of the hidden God, who is praying in all creation and in all persons. Because it is supported by a variety of social and ritual structures, communal prayer is easier to sustain than personal prayer. But it is difficult to approach God as the Divine Beloved in public prayer. We need opportunities for private prayer that can express our devotion and affection for God. Private prayer, when it is truly a communion with God, will always lead us into communal prayer. When we come to times of communal prayer, with our family or with the parish, our having prayed privately will nourish and enrich the communal expression. The prayer of the community, while rich and deep, can never be a total substitute for personal prayer and can never be complete unless each member carries to it his or her own individual prayer.

All true prayer leads us outward from the center of ourselves. All true prayer leads to social justice and apostolic labor. But without personal prayer, social action is hollow. Without a meditative heart, social reform can easily become self-glorifying instead of an act that gives glory to God. The coming of the Kingdom must begin with a heart that is praying always and always reforming.

SPECIAL NOTE: *The following daily prayers begin and end with the instruction: "sacred gesture." This can be a profound bow of the head or body or a sign of the cross. This sacred action should be done slowly and with devotion. The instruction "sacred gesture" after the examination of conscience and prayer of forgiveness can be the sign of the cross, a profound bow or dipping one's hands in a bowl of water as a sign of cleansing.*

Some sections of the daily prayers in which special intentions are offered are set off with brackets. These sections may be omitted when read aloud in a group. Individuals who use the prayer forms, however, are encouraged to regularly include specific personal intentions in their times of prayer, as well as lifting up in prayer the needs of family, friends, neighbors and the larger local and even world communities in order to foster an awareness of the interconnection of us all.

CANTICLE
OF CREATION

In the beginning, Lord God,
    You alone existed: eternally one
    yet pregnant in the fullness of unity.
Full to overflowing,
    You, Father of All Life, exploded outward
    in a billion bits and pieces.

Your Words became flesh,
    whirling in shining stars, shimmering suns
    and in genesis glimmering galaxies.
You, my God, spoke,
    and Your Words became flesh:
    in sun and moon, earth and seas,
    mountains and gentle hills,
    rolling rivers and silent streams.
You, my God, spoke,
    and Your Words became flesh:
    in winged bird, in deer and elephant,
    in grazing cow, racing horse and fish of the deep.
Your Words, so unique and so varied,
    filled the earth also with rabbit, squirrel and ant.
And all Your Words were beautiful,
    and all were good.

From each of these holy Words
    arose a prayer of praise and adoration
    to You, their creator
    and wondrous womb.

"Praise You," rang out the redwood,
> "Blessed be You," chimed in the cedar,
> "Holy are You," prayed the prairie grasses.

From all four corners of this earth,
> rose up a chorus of perpetual adoration.

O Sacred Spirit, O Divine Breath of Life,
> unseal my ears that they may ever listen
> to Your continuous canticle of creation;
> open my heart and my whole self,
> to sing in harmony with all its many voices.

Teach me to commune with Your first Word made flesh,
> Your Creation,
> that I may be able to unravel the wondrous words
> of Your second Word made flesh,
> Jesus,
> through whom, with whom and in whom,
> I may see myself as another Word of Yours made flesh,
> to Your glory and honor.

Amen✝

SUNDAY MORNING PRAYER

sacred gesture

Lord God, Creator of All That Is,
    a graceful salutation to You,
    who are gloriously present in all the earth,
    in the heavens and in that undiscovered beyond.
I bow before You and adore You.

You are the Source of Light whose day star, the sun,
    has joyfully announced the beginning of a new day.
This is the first day of the week;
    at sunrise, on such a day as this,
    Your Son, Jesus, rose from the tomb by Your holy
      power.
This day is holy; may I be holy together with it.
May this morning prayer of mine, simple and silent,
    be joined with the prayers of all Your people
    that rise to You today.

period of silent prayer or meditation

I unite myself with all who are at worship on this
    Sunday
    as I read this Gospel passage
    (from today's Eucharistic Celebration).

reading from the Gospels

a psalm or spoken prayer

I rejoice, my Lord and Beloved Giver of Gifts,
    in all the possibilities of this new week that begins
    today.

I am glad for the chance to rest from my usual labors
and to take pleasure in this day.
In this holy leisure,
I shall pattern myself upon You, my Lord God,
when, on such a day as this,
You sat back and enjoyed the work of Your hands.
May I prayerfully and playfully waste time today
and so give You glory and honor.
I pause before I begin my daily activities
to pray for my special intentions: _____
(and I also remember the special intentions of:

_____).
Lord, may all the earth be at peace this Sunday morning.

O Lord of the Universe,
O Divine Spirit of Creation,
O Jesus, Lord and Holy Pattern for my life;
forever and ever, I bow to You.

sacred gesture

Sunday Evening Prayer

sacred gesture

My Lord, I lift up my heart to You
    at the end of this day of rest and worship.
This has been a day of the sun
    and of the Son of God
    whose resurrection from the dead we have
        remembered.
As I come to the conclusion of this sacred day,
    I pause to give You praise and to thank You
    for all the good things that it has held for me.

pause for silent reflection

If I have failed to drink in the wondrous possibilities
    of such a special and holy day,
    I am sorry;
    for this and for all failings, I ask Your pardon.

pause for silent reflection and sacred gesture

Holy is this day;
    may my prayer of stillness
    be saturated with its sacred splendor
    as I now enter into silence.

period of silent prayer or meditation

a psalm, spiritual reading or spoken prayer

Lord of All Days,
    of Sundays and weekdays,

as this first day of the week now draws to a close,
   I thank You for Your continuous presence.
Renewed and re-created by this holy day,
      may I be willing to embrace all You have prepared
         for me
      in tomorrow's return to the routine of daily life.

I pause and pray for my special intentions: _____,
      and I remember in prayer the needs of my family
      and of all those whom I love.
(In particular, I remember the needs of: _____.)
I reach out tonight and touch them with the kiss of
      peace,
      and I surrender to sleep and to Your divine
         embrace.

Lord of Day and Night, of Life and Death,
   I place myself into Your holy hands.

   sacred gesture

MONDAY MORNING PRAYER

sacred gesture

Lord my God,
    the morning sky announces a new day.
All around me, creation is beginning its song of praise.
I now join my heart and body
    with all peoples and all creation
    as I lift up my heart to You, my God.

This day will hold much for me,
    and so that I may not miss its hidden message,
    Your living word to me,
    I now enter the cave of my heart
    and, there, pray to You in stillness.
Quiet of body and peaceful of spirit,
    I rest in You.

period of silent prayer or meditation

My Lord,
    You shall speak to me
    in the events of this new day that is beginning.
You have spoken in the past through Your holy ones;
    may this spiritual reflection be food for me this day.

a psalm, spiritual reading or spoken prayer

Renewed, my Lord and God,
    in the freshness of this morning hour,
    I can now go forth with a graceful heart
    and a peaceful spirit.
Mindful of my daily need before You,
    I pray for my personal intentions: _____.

My needs also include the happiness and peace of
    others,
    so I also lift up to You, my God,
    the needs, this day,
    (of_____, and those)
    of all the earth as well.

O Lord of the Universe,
    O Divine Spirit of Creation,
    O Jesus, Lord and Holy Pattern for my life;
    forever and ever, I bow to You.

    sacred gesture

Monday Evening Prayer

sacred gesture

This day, a gift from You, my Lord, is ending.
As the veil of evening is drawn across the sky,
    I look back over the activities of this day
    with gratitude and with an eye for sin.
First, I pause in gratitude for all that has happened
    to me.

pause for silent reflection

If I have been the cause of pain to another,
    if I have forgotten others' needs
    in my hurry to serve my own,
    I am sorry.
May the words of Jesus
    be a lamp for me to examine this day.

pause for silent reflection

My God, I willingly forgive all who have injured me
    and ask their forgiveness at the end of this day.
May Your divine absolution
    cleanse me of any sin or failing.

sacred gesture

Surrounded by Your Divine Presence,
    in union with all whom I love and all who love You,
    I enter into stillness.

period of silent prayer or meditation

Lord of Night, Creator of the Stars and the Moon,
    I thank You for the graceful gifts of this day.
May the problems and pains of today be healed
    as I surrender myself to Your nightly care.
I rest in You, Divine Friend and Companion,
    who watches over me while I sleep.
Bless, this evening, those whom I love
    (and watch, in a special way, over_____)
    and all who suffer this night.
Lord of Day and Night, of life and Death,
    I place myself into Your holy hands.

sacred gesture

TUESDAY MORNING PRAYER

sacred gesture

Lord my God,
>   I have risen from the prayer of death, from my
>   sleep,
>   and now share in that daily resurrection called
>   dawn.
May I, by this time of communion with You,
>   once again set my feet to the path of holiness.

The light of this new day touches all things,
>   touches trees, grass, hills and all the earth.
In all the events of this day,
>   Your Divine Light, O God, will touch all
>   as it shines forth from within Your creation.
Lord, grant that I may see.

I join myself now
>   with all who seek You in truth and purity of heart
>   as I enter into the prayer of stillness.

period of silent prayer or meditation

God of Truth,
>   You have spoken in the past in the sacred writings,
>   and You continue to speak today in the events of
>   life.
May I hear Your special word for me in this spiritual
>   reflection.

a psalm, spiritual reading or spoken prayer

Lord of the Dawn,
>> my heart has opened in this time of communion
>> with You.
I ask that I may spend this entire day
>> in the spirit of this time of prayer.
May my efforts to walk in the footsteps of Your Son,
Jesus,
>> make my actions, words and thoughts all be holy.
Aware of how easy it is to lose the Way,
>> I now pray for my personal needs: _____,
>> (and I lift up the special needs of: _____)
>> and the needs of all the earthen family to which I
>> belong.

O Lord of the Universe,
>> O Divine Spirit of Creation,
>> O Jesus, Lord and Holy Pattern for my life;
>> forever and ever, I bow to You.

> *sacred gesture*

Tuesday Evening Prayer

sacred gesture

Lord my God, this day is ending.
Your daughter, darkness,
    comes to wrap me in her embrace,
    and I seek to be embraced by You, my Loving Lord.
I pause to thank You for the multitude of gifts
    that have come to me from You, the Lord of Life.

pause for silent reflection

Divided, I cannot pray.
If I, by word or action, have divided myself from others,
    I wish to be sorry.
Remove from my heart any sin
    for which I may have been responsible this day.

pause for silent reflection and sacred gesture

The temple of the heart now cleansed,
    I enter, with devotion,
    into stillness and communion with You, my God.

period of silent prayer or meditation

a psalm, spiritual reading or spoken prayer

Blessed are You, Lord my God, who never slumbers
    but keeps vigil over all creation.
Shield me this night from all that is evil.
May the lamp of gratitude that burns within my heart,
    lighting upon the many gifts of this day and of my
        life,
    be for me a night-long guard.

I lift up into Your Divine Heart these needs: _____.
Bless, this night, all those whom I love,
    (as I remember the special needs of_____)
    and care for the needs of all the earth.

Lord of Day and Night, of Life and Death,
    I place myself into Your holy hands.

   sacred gesture

Wednesday Morning Prayer

sacred gesture

Lord my God,
> like the rest of creation at the beginning of this day,
> I am not yet fully awake.
Open not only my eyes,
> but awaken my heart
> to the mystery of Your Divine Presence in all the
> earth.
I arise to meet the challenges of this day in my work.
I arise to greet the surprises
> hidden in the hours of this fresh and new day.
I arise also to embrace the mystery of the Cross of
> Christ
> which awaits me in the troubles of today.
I join myself with all of those who love You and seek
> You
> regardless of their race or creed.
In that holy unity, I enter into stillness.

period of silent prayer or meditation

a psalm, spiritual reading or spoken prayer

Lord, as the light of the sun pushes back the darkness of
> night
> to reveal a wondrous world,
> may my small steps along the way of Your Son,
> Jesus,
> reveal Your Light to all I will meet.

May this time of prayer
>grant me the grace to face all that shall happen this
>>day
>as part of Your special plan for me.
Let me fill my pockets with the hidden gifts
>concealed within my work, my family and my life.
May I reject no single one of them because of failing to
>>see
>the word or event, the pleasure or pain
>as holding Your holy meaning.
I now pray for my special personal needs: _____;
>(I remember in my prayer the needs of_____)
>and all the needs of our earth.

O Lord of the Universe,
>O Divine Spirit of Creation,
>O Jesus, Lord and Holy Pattern for my life;
>forever and ever, I bow to You.

>*sacred gesture*

WEDNESDAY EVENING PRAYER

sacred gesture

Lord, Divine Keeper of All Time,
   the hours of this day that remain are few;
   night is upon me.
Touch my memory
   and make me aware of today's gifts.

pause for silent reflection

The redemption of the world,
   the removal of injustice
   and the spread of unity among all peoples
   is beyond my limited abilities.
Lord, help me to examine
   how I have failed to redeem that small part of
      the world
   that did touch my life today.

pause for silent reflection and sacred gesture

In that holy unity,
   with my heart at peace and surrounded with
      gratitude,
   I now enter into a sacred stillness.

period of silent prayer or meditation

a psalm, spiritual reading or spoken prayer

Beloved Lord, I rejoice in Your Mystic Presence.
In ten thousand ways,
   You have been present in ordinary events this day.

You have waited, in patience, in those persons and times
in which I failed to be aware of Your Divine
Presence.
Tomorrow, my Lord,
I shall see more,
and I shall be open-eyed so as not to miss You.

You, my Lord, know all our needs,
but I am mindful of my poverty before You
and therefore lift up to You
the needs that are in my heart tonight: _____.
I lift up to Your Divine Heart

all those who at the end of this day
are without shelter or food.
Be with them and with all the earth this night.
May I sleep in peace and awaken to life.

Lord of Day and Night, of Life and Death,
I place myself into Your holy hands.

sacred gesture

sacred gesture

My Lord and my God,
    a new day has come to my door,
    fresh and full of life.
With gratitude and a sense of wonder,
    I greet this day and You, my God.
The sacrament of sleep has healed my heart
    and granted strength to my body.

My cousins in creation—
    trees, birds, fish and four-legged creatures—
    are arising with a song of adoration.
I desire to join my prayer with theirs.
May my simple praises be in harmony
    with the songs of the wind and the earth,
    as I now enter into the prayer of stillness.

period of silent prayer or meditation

a psalm, spiritual reading or spoken prayer

My Lord and God,
    as Your Son, Jesus, found Your Sacred Presence
    not only in the Temple
    but also within the temple of the cosmos,
    may I find You in everything and everyone I meet.
He, who is our savior and teacher, sought You, His
Father,
    in mountain heights and desert wastes,

in the faces of His neighbors
and in the laughter of His companions.
May I who walk in His footsteps do the same this day.
In this spirit, I now pray for my personal needs:

_____

(and for the needs of others: _____).
May I listen today to the prayers
of wind, earth, lakes and rivers, and all that grows.
With Your holy help, I shall live prayerfully
in harmony with that continuous
and blessed prayer of Your creation.

226   O Lord of the Universe,
O Divine Spirit of Creation,
O Jesus, Lord and Holy Pattern for my life;
forever and ever, I bow to You.

sacred gesture

Thursday Evening Prayer

sacred gesture

My Lord, Beloved Source of All That Is,
    I bow before You as I come to the end of my day.
The sun has journeyed across the sky
    and has disappeared beneath the horizon.
This day is now complete,
    and I greet the darkness of night
    with a prayer of gratitude.
I thank You for all the sun-touched gifts of this day.

pause for silent reflection

I ask Your mercy for the times, this day,
    when I have forgotten to be kind and compassionate.
I am sorry for the times
    when I have rushed through the mystery of life,
    blind to the needs of others
    or to the beauties of creation.

pause for silent reflection and sacred gesture

In a communion with stars, planets and moons,
    in communion with all the servants of God,
    may I enter into sacred stillness.

period of silent prayer or meditation

a psalm, spiritual reading or spoken prayer

My Lord and God,
    Cosmic Creator of both the Sun and Moon,
    I praise and adore You.

In divine wisdom, You have balanced all of creation,
    day and night, male and female,
    summer and winter, light and dark.
I embrace that balance
    and, in this day that is closing,
    have attempted to balance the needs of body and
        spirit,
    the demands of the inner person and the public
        person.
Wrapped in gratitude,
    I now place before You my personal needs:

    _____

    (as well as the needs of others: _____).

Lord of Day and Night, of Life and Death,
    I place myself into Your holy hands.

    sacred gesture

FRIDAY MORNING PRAYER

sacred gesture

My Lord and my God,
>   I seek to begin this day in union with You
>   and with all of those I love.
All around me, the world is waking
>   and preparing to begin the work of this day.
Soon I must take into my hands
>   the various duties of my life.
The sun fills the eastern sky with light
>   as once again I prepare to make all this day shall
>>   contain
>   part of the fabric of my prayer.
Before I do, I bow before You and ask Your divine
>   assistance.

In a holy harmony with all the earth,
>   with all peoples and with those I love,
>   I enter into the prayer of stillness.

period of silent prayer or meditation

My Lord, grant me sacred vision
>   to read between the words of this spiritual reflection
>   and so to find those messages
>   that You have left especially for me.

a psalm, spiritual reading or spoken prayer

My Lord and God, it is already Friday.
The week is passing quickly as does all of life.
Awaken me this morning
>   so that I shall not waste anything of life this day.

As Jesus, Your Son, on a Friday
    embraced suffering and death upon His cross,
    may I take up my cross
    and use it as a ladder to climb into Your Divine
      Heart.
Mindful of the challenge of that cross
    with which You have gifted me in life,
    I now pray for my personal needs: _____ ,
    (and for the special needs of_____)
    as well as the many needs of all the earth and its
      people.

230   O Lord of the Universe,
    O Divine Spirit of Creation,
    O Jesus, Lord and Holy Pattern for my life;
    forever and ever, I bow to You.

    sacred gesture

sacred gesture

My Lord and my God, hear my prayer
    as I prepare to close the door of this day.
I know, my Lord, that nothing happens by accident in life.
May I, therefore, with the gift of memory, walk through
    my day
    and touch with gratitude all that has happened to me.

pause for silent reflection

The cost of redemption was great:
    the pain and suffering of Your Son, Jesus.
I am sorry if my sins of this day,
    the failings of thoughtlessness,
    the neglect caused by my selfishness,
    have wounded the world and myself as well.
Heal me of all failings.

pause for silent reflection and sacred gesture

Escorted by the spirits of gratitude and pardon,
    I enter the temple of my heart
    and bow before Your Divine Presence.

period of silent prayer or meditation

a psalm, spiritual reading or spoken prayer

My Lord, my Beloved,
    I prepare to let go of my control of today.
Soon sleep will close my eyes and empty my hands of
    work.

Each time this happens,
    I practice my departure into death.
May this sacrament of sleep
    teach me not to fear death but to trust
    in Your abounding affection and compassionate
      care,
    for I sleep in You.
I lift up into Your Divine Heart
    the intentions that have been in my heart this day:

    _____.

I pray to You with confidence,

    since I pray in the name of Your Son, Jesus,
    who died in Your arms,
    only to be rescued from the tomb
    in the eternal dawn of the Resurrection.

Lord of Day and Night, of Life and Death,
    I place myself into Your holy hands.

    sacred gesture

Saturday Morning Prayer

sacred gesture

My Lord and my God,
    the sun has risen to open the last day of this week.
May this, the seventh day, be one of prayer and praise
    and be filled with Your Divine Light.

Whatever this day holds behind its back, unseen by
    me—
    be it play or work, treasures or troubles, rain or
      shine—
    may I taste each of this day's gifts with zest.

In a harmony of sky and earth,
    in a communion of life
    that encompasses all the world and all peoples,
    I now enter into sacred stillness.

period of silent prayer or meditation

May I hear Your personal revelation to me
    in the words of this spiritual reflection,
    and may it accompany me this day
    and teach me of the mysteries of Your love.

a psalm, spiritual reading or spoken prayer

My Lord and my God,
    may Your holiness be made visible to me this day.
May every bush be aflame,
    glowing brilliantly with Your splendor.
Your voice has echoed in the prophets
    and in the lives of saints;

all of creation rings in Your divine resonance.
May my ears be in tune with that echo,
    and my heart be shaped by its secrets.
I pray for my personal intentions: _____,
        (and for the needs of_____)
    as well as the numerous needs of all this earth.

O Lord of the Universe,
    O Divine Spirit of Creation,
    O Jesus, Lord and Holy Pattern for my life;
    forever and ever, I bow to You.

sacred gesture

sacred gesture

My Lord, this day is ending
    and with it a week of seven days,
    a week of seven holy days filled with Your Divine
      Presence.
How can I ask You to gift me with a new week of days
    unless I am grateful for all the gifts of life
    in this week that is ending?
I pause now and thankfully remember
    the history of this past week, beginning with
      Monday.

    pause for silent reflection on the seven days of the week
    (This reflection will be longer and more thoughtful than
    usual for an evening prayer.)

I desire to greet this new week with freshness.
Come, Lord, and remove all the grime and sin
    of this day and week now ending.
With the lamp of truth,
    I carefully explore the passages of my heart.

    pause for silent reflection and sacred gesture

Peaceful, pardoned, with a heart full of gratitude,
    I enter now into silent prayer.

    period of silent prayer or meditation

    a psalm, spiritual reading or spoken prayer

My Lord,
    like a watchful guard,

I await the coming of a new day, Sunday,
the gateway of a new week.
I am filled with trust for whatever awaits me in this
week.
Nourished by that trust,
I pray for my special intentions: _____.
May Your holy spirits stand guard over my sleep
so that I may rest peacefully
and rise in abounding hope.

Lord of Day and Night, of Life and Death,
I place myself into Your holy hands.

sacred gesture

THE SAMARITAN PRAYER, FOR SOMEONE TOO BUSY TO PRAY

Lord my God,
> You may have missed me today,
> > since I did not have time to kneel and pray.
I did pray, my Lord,
> but not the usual prayer of my day.
Instead, I prayed the prayer of the Samaritan.

You see, my Lord,
> my neighbor was in need:
> I saw the trouble, heard the cry for help.
In my neighbor's need, I saw You in need.
In my neighbor's plea for help,
> I heard a call to prayer
> and could not pass by.
May this helping-prayer
> truly be my prayer this day.
For in the midst of the difficulty,
> I felt Your Sacred Presence.
I tasted the flavor of communion
> in all that happened between us.

So my Lord,
> while absent from formal prayer,
> I was present
> to You and to my neighbor,
> in this my Samaritan prayer.

While I was unable to say my prayers,
    I thank You for the gift of *being* prayer.
May all the spoken prayers of my life
        prepare me to be always ready
        to pray the helping-prayer
        and provide me with the grace
        to be the Emmanuel prayer.

Blessed are You, Lord our God,
        who gifts us with the opportunities
        to pray the Samaritan prayer
        of compassionate concern.

Amen✝

RECONCILIATION
WITHIN
THE
HOME

mong the multitude of all the gifts in God's creation, communion is one of the most beautiful
to have come from the divine hand.
Communion is the fruit of love and is the life-spirit of the
home. It consists of a delicate balance between the experience of self and the experience of the other. However, an
imbalance can easily be produced, ushering into our lives
pain and suffering by the absence of communion. Therefore,
one of the most frequently needed rituals in the home is
that of reconciliation. Our Lord Jesus, mindful of this need,
again and again reminded His disciples that they were to forgive one another continuously. He went so far as to say that
God would forgive us our sins in the manner in which we
forgive each other's. Holy, then, within the Church is the
sacrament of the healing of hearts, the sacrament of
Penance. By its grace, we are united with each other, with
God and with all the members of the Body of Christ as our
sins are forgiven. The words of our Lord also speak of a
human ritual that is a preface to the sacrament of Penance
when He said that we are to go to the one whom we have
offended and seek forgiveness before we come to the altar
with our gifts. This one-to-one ritual is part of the healing
mystery of forgiveness. Among the numerous rituals of the

domestic church, this one of reconciliation is the most difficult to perform, but also the most necessary!

Prayer, sacrifice and worship are impossible if we are
divided from one another, and, therefore, from God. Hate,
division and anger poison our hearts and open the door to
disease and to sickness. The inner-person cannot be sick for
long without the whole person falling ill. Sin is a spreading
sickness of the spirit and demands prompt healing. To deal
with it, we need a passion for communion, a passion so great
that we will not fear the painful work of reconciliation. In
this work, we shall need prayerful time, space and reflection
to examine our wounds. We shall need grace and encouragement to search our hearts for the ways in which each of us
involved is responsible for any separation. We shall need
special grace so that the ceremony of reunion will not turn
into another battleground for more pain and personal
injury. We should always come to the peace table unarmed!
We should approach reunion with a resolve not to reach
back in history for a weapon of past offense, for some old
hurt with which to hurl new pain at the other. From beginning to end, the prayer of reconciliation within our homes
demands the presence of the All Holy One.

Whatever form this reconciliation may take, we should
reverence the place where we, carrying our sins with us, meet
with God and one another for a return to communion. The
actual sign of absolution may be an embrace or a kiss, a
handshake or even a good laugh. These signs, as well as the
work and pain that are part of the prayer, are sacred.

Daily and in different ways we may come to one another
asking to be forgiven. Some are as simple as "excuse me" or
"I'm sorry, dear, that I was late," while others demand more
time and prayer. In times when the separation is deep, we
need the grace of God so that we will act justly and with
compassion toward the other person. The prayers of this
part of our handbook are intended to be of assistance in
this holy and human work of reconciliation. Let us keep

in mind that every act of forgiveness can be for us a holy communion. Each time we forgive one another is a blessing. Each time we forgive one another is part of the healing of the sin of the world.

Within the home, the ritual of forgiveness can flow in all directions.

All persons of all ages can be ministers of this domestic sacrament of reunion. Parents should never hesitate to ask the pardon of their children if their behavior as parents has been unjust or wrong. Children should ask the forgiveness of their brothers and sisters for the nicks and scratches of daily life and the pardon of their parents when their words or actions have been the cause of pain or separation.

Once we have met one another in humility and forgiveness at the peace table, then we can come to the table of the Eucharist without guilt. When communion has been restored, then we can experience this sacred sacrament of the Church with true fruitfulness.

Every sin has its effect upon the home which then ripples out to the far shores of the earth. In like fashion, every act of pardon and reunion restores peace and health not only to the home but, in a very real way, to the whole world as well. This prayer of pardon which leads to full communion has truly cosmic consequences and is, therefore, among the most sacred of all our prayers.

Lord, You who expressed Your divine anger
    in fire, brimstone and lightning,
    look down with understanding upon my anger.
I am in pain;
    a wound in my heart caused by another
    is the source of this suffering.
That heart of mine, Lord of Hearts, is filled with anger
    so that I am unable to be loving and caring.
I feel a need to return injury for injury, pain for pain,
    and so cannot truly desire to forgive the other.
Lord, You and I both know that such an attitude is
    wrong;
    yet it is very real,
    and its pain overflows into the rest of my life.
Before I can come to the point of wanting to forgive—
    and to be forgiven if that is necessary—
    I must find an antidote for the poison of this
      attitude.
Lord, I need Your help, for my feelings are confused,
    and I so need to find some order among them.
I need to see how this separation has come about
    and how I can take some steps
    toward mending my broken communion.
I pause now to exchange places

and to look at the cause of the separation
through the eyes of the other who has injured me.

pause for silent examination

Lord, You who are a God of compassion as well as holy
   anger,
   may I see how that which angers me in the other
   is also a part of my person which I repel.
Help me to own that part of me
   and thus begin to know my oneness with the other.
May this passover of mine to the other's side
   make me ready for a solution to this division,
   and may my desire for communion
   soak up the poison in my heart.
Lead me, Forgiving Lord, to the graces of reconciliation
   so that this relationship which is dead
   may be resurrected to fuller life
   through Your holy and healing power.

Ament

My God, You who perpetually pardon
    all who are sincere in their sorrow,
    help me as I seek to forgive myself.
I realize, my Lord, that unless I can forgive myself
    I cannot fully forgive those who have offended me.
Humble my heart
    so that I can embrace all that is hidden within me.

You, Lord of Creation,
    have divided time into day and night.
My life is likewise divided
    between light and darkness,
    good and bad.
When these dark, negative needs are excessive
    and out of balance with the positive,
    they become destructive to others,
    and to myself as well.

I forgive myself for becoming impatient
    because I was too busy, too particular or in a hurry.
I forgive myself for this failing
    as I forgive others who are impatient, too.
I forgive myself for making mistakes,
    for being too quick to act or to speak,
    for not taking time to think;

I forgive myself as well as others
who make their own mistakes.
I forgive myself for being stupid in sinning, for falling
into
the same errors which injure others and myself.
I forgive myself for those small sins
that irritate others and cause me shame.
For a smallness of mind in my thoughts,
for a narrowness of heart in my actions,
I forgive myself
and forgive others who act and think as do I.

Compassionate Lord, I know how I sin most easily;
help me to understand and to correct this failing.

A pause for silent reflection may be used here.

I grant myself pardon and forgiveness
so that my darkness may fuel the goodness
within me,
a goodness which You, my God,
have placed in great deposit within me.

Amen✝

Come, Lord of Healing and Unity,
    I am in need of Your divine assistance.
I need to approach another
    and to find a way to peace and understanding.
We are now separated,
    and the canyon between us is painful and empty of
      You.
Help me to be honest as I seek reunion.
Open to my vision the ways by which I have failed
    and have been lacking in consideration.
Let my heart be ready to see how I have sinned.
I will need Your help
    so that I may move beyond my own feelings
    to an awareness of the other who is also suffering.

You, Searcher of Hearts,
    know how both of us in our own ways
    are at fault.
Teach us to be humble
    as we seek reunion.
Come and stand between us
    so that all we say and do
    will be filled with the sacred medicine of heaven.
Remind us how short our lives are
    so that we will not delay this reunion of hearts.

Inspire us to see how this separation
    can serve to bring us even closer together,
    closer than we were before it happened.
Most of all, Lord of Compassion,
    let me be a servant of pardon,
    a minister of reconciliation,
    as I now pray for Your holy guidance.

pause for silent prayer

Lord, Divine Parent,
    make me as humble and healing as our mother the
        earth.
Make me as honest and defenseless as a child.
Make me as compassionate and loving as Your Son,
    Jesus.
And, Lord and Giver of True Strength,
    make me as forgiving as are You, Yourself.

Amen✝

Lord God, Just Judge and Compassionate Holy Parent,
    be here with us
    as we seek to be re-united in reconciliation
    after a time of separation.
We pause now to be aware of Your Sacred Presence
    among us.

   pause for silent prayer

We come together in Your Holy Presence
    as we seek to forget the past and its mistakes
    and to be once again united in love.
We remember the story told by Your Son and our Lord,
    Jesus,
    about the son who had left home and sinned,
    and yet his father was eager and anxious to embrace
        him
    and to celebrate his return.
Mindful of the deep meanings in that beautiful story,
    we too are anxious that old scars be healed
    and that rejoicing once again fill our lives.
We forgive one another
    for any way in which we have caused pain to one
        another
    or may have torn apart the fabric of our unity
    by this injury.

Lord, You truly know
    that we all make mistakes and have failed;

look upon us who have been offended
and lift our hearts;
look upon us who have given offense
and help us heal the hurt of our actions and words.

As we willingly forgive one another,
forgive us our sins as well
and fill us with Your healing power and grace.

Lord, we lack a fattened calf with which to celebrate,
but may the spirit of feasting and dancing
fill our hearts now made new
by Your healing grace of forgiveness.

As we embrace each other,
may we be enveloped by You, our Lord and God,
and united in peace and in love.

Amen†

250

Come close, Lord, and hear my prayer
    as I come with great hesitation
    seeking reconciliation with You, my God.
I find that my lips will hardly form these words,
    and yet, if I am honest, I know that at times
    there has been hidden in my heart
    a resentment toward You, my God.
The reason, Lord, is that from the start
    You have shaped my world,
    formed my body, gifted my mind
    and placed me within my family.
I have held You responsible when these seemed unjust
    and, though afraid,
    have often wanted to raise my fist to You.
This, Lord God, is one of those times!

Be patient with me, Divine Master,
    because from the spot where I stand,
    I can see only a small part of this universe.
My vision is confined
    to a limited today, to a few yesterdays.
I cannot grasp the full sweep of Your divine plan,
    of which my life is a tiny but important part.

I know in my heart of hearts
    that You love me without limit
    and that You desire

only that which is good and wholesome for me.
With that knowledge,
    I can embrace, without understanding it all,
    what You have decreed for me from all time.
I embrace my body, my family,
    my place in history and even this present situation
    for which I can see no simple resolution.

Lord God, please accept my pardon
    and embrace me with Your divine affection.
Smile upon my simple efforts to serve and praise You
    even as I sometimes stumble through my life.

Thank You, my Lord and my Friend,
    for Your patience
    and Your gracious acceptance of my forgiveness.
May we live together forever.

Amen†

Times
of
Sickness

Into all our lives comes the mystery of illness and pain. This veiled visitor, sickness, should always be greeted with prayer. The American Hopi Indians believed that medicine should never be given to a sick person unless prayer is also given. They recognized the profound relationship between physical health and that of the inner-person and the relationship between our human lives and the Divine Mystery.

Illness can come to us personally or to a member of our family or a close friend. When sickness comes to our family, it is an occasion to join our hearts in prayer for the healing of the sick person, whether child or adult. When we ourselves or members of our family are sick and need medicine, like the Hopi, we too should let that medicine be accompanied by our faith-filled prayer.

After we have recovered through prayer, medical care, and rest, we can lift up our hearts in gratitude for the gift of health. This gesture can be not only a prayer of gratitude but also of rededication to seeking a constant condition of good health through proper diet, rest, recreation and prayerful living.

Often, we are asked to pray for a friend or member of the family who is sick. This prayer allows us to encircle the sick person with the power of God as well as with our own love and affection. By praying in times of sickness, we can become more conscious of our interdependency upon one another as well as of our intimate relationship with God.

To turn, at times of illness, only to medical science, even with all of its marvelous gifts and knowledge, is to treat only half the person. By prayer and medicine, we do indeed find what the American Indians called "good medicine," a healing for body and soul.

BLESSING PRAYER
IN A TIME OF SICKNESS

Lord of Health and Wholeness,
    in Your divine plan, You have seen fit
    to include, within Your marvelous creation,
    disease and sickness.
Life becomes a balance of sickness and health,
    just as time is balanced between night and day.

Your servant (*name*) now lies sick
    and desires to be restored
    to the balance of good health.
Hear, O Lord, our prayers
    for the healing of him/her whom we love so much.

Remove from him/her this illness
    so that, fully recovered and restored to health,
    he/she may return with renewed zeal
    to the daily life that we share.
We trust fully in the Divine Power
    to stir the hidden healing powers of the body.
So awakened, these God-given powers
    will remove all that causes pain and sickness.

addressing the sick person:

With abounding hope and faith,
    we now place our hands upon you
    as we call forth the healing medicine of God's grace.

*Persons praying may lay hands on the sick person and pray
in silence.*

Divine Healer and Lord of Wholeness,
together we place ourselves in Your hands.
We ask for healing
but also for acceptance of Your holy plan for each
of us.
Help us to embrace
whatever You have decreed for _(name)_;
assist him/her in the acceptance of this sickness
as You support him/her
with the strength of Your Holy Spirit.

addressing the sick person:

May you be blessed
with the power and the love of God
and the affection of those who love you.

Amen✝

_The sick person may be signed with the sign of the cross
and may also be kissed._

Prayer
to Accompany the
Taking of Medicine

Lord,
    my sickness has made praying difficult.
Its pain makes me self-conscious,
    so that I find it a burden
    to think of the needs of others.
Divine Healer, I need Your aid.

May this medicine
    which I am about to take
    cure me and call forth
    the hidden healing powers of my body.

The medicine is taken.

I ask that through the power of the Cross of Christ,
    this medicine, blended with faith and devotion,
    may restore me to the fullness of health.

A sign of the cross or other sacred gesture is made.

Lord, with faith and abounding hope in Your love,
    I pray in communion with You, my Beloved,
    and with all those who desire my healing,
    my return to the wholeness of health.
I place trust in this medicine
    based on my trust in You,
    the eternal healing medicine of life.
I believe in Your holy power to heal me
    of all that has combined to create my present
        illness.

I seek to be healed,
> but I seek even more Your holy will
> as I embrace Your final choice.

Bowing in loving obedience
> as did Your Son, Jesus, on the Mount of Olives,
> I seek holiness in Your will
> more than just health of body.

Amen✝

Prayer of Gratitude for Having Been Restored to Health

Lord of All Gifts
    and God who hears our prayers,
    I come with a full heart to thank You
    that I have been healed of my sickness.
I remember the stories of those
    whom Your Son, Jesus, cured:
        of how they danced, rejoiced and proclaimed Your
        glory.
I too, in this prayer of gratitude,
    dance with delight
    that my sickness has passed.

I am grateful that You,
    the designer and creator of the human body,
    have placed within it a network of healing
    by which it can rebuild and restore itself.
I am thankful that this inner-system of restoration
    has been aided by the marvel of modern healing
    methods.
But I am most grateful
    that Your divine power has overshadowed me
    and used these natural and human means
    to remove my sickness.

Now reunited to the flow of daily life,
    may I express my gratitude day by day
    in a proper care for my body and its health.

May I, by rest and recreation,
   keep my body whole and healthy.
Grant to me, Lord,
   the grace to also be sensitive
   to those who are sick.
May I be aware of their pain
   and respond to their needs of support and prayer.

Lord, may my prayerful gratitude be shown
   in my enjoyment of life,
   in my care
   for the often overlooked gift of good health
   and be most clearly shown in my devoted service
   to You and to all Your creation.

Blessed are You, Lord our God,
   who heals and saves Your people.

Amen✝

Lord our God, hear our prayer as we come before You.
Your servant (*name*) is sick
    and is in need of our affection
    and prayerful support.

We pause now and, in silence, pray for his/her recovery.

    pause for silent prayer

We pray for those who love (*name*)
    and who surround him/her in this time of sickness.
Support them
    with the sacred strength of Your Spirit
    so that by their love
    they may be medicine for the healing of our friend.

May this sickness be for us a cause of gratitude,
    we who are enjoying the fruits of good health.
As we pray for our friend,
    may we also thank You
    for this fragile gift of health
    that we possess by Your holy will.

Lord, in the communion of love,
    we now reach out (across the miles)
    and surround the bed and the body of (*name*)
    with light, love and the power of prayer.

    pause for silent prayer

Healing, health and holiness be his/hers.
May peace, grace and love surround him/her
    and an awareness of Your Divine Presence
    be a tent over his/her bed of pain.

Blessed are You, Lord and God,
    who rescues those You love
    from pain and sickness.

Amen†

THE SHADOW
OF
DEATH
ACROSS
THE
HOME

M any years ago, before the age of instant global communications, the news of death that reached a home was limited. The family learned only of the death of a family member, a neighbor, a member of the parish or on certain occasions the death of some famous person. Today, the family hears the news of death as it comes upon persons all over our earth. The daily newspaper, the television, and the Internet constantly bring into the home the latest reports of terrorism, war, famine, police shoot-outs, and highway accidents, making death as common as the weather. In almost all of these cases, we do not know the people who have died. Nameless to us, their deaths do not very deeply touch our lives.

Certainly, the news of death has an effect upon us, but we seem to be numbed by the constant news of death on a global scale. We suffer from an overexposure to the message that death has visited our world. As a result, the announcement of death often calls forth little emotion from us. Psychologically, we cannot be involved on such a worldwide scale, and so our impersonal reaction to the news of death received through the media is understandable. When a neighbor or fellow worker dies, the danger is that our response will be conditioned by this over-exposure. The danger is that we shall respond to the news with a reflex-like comment of regret and then move on with the normal business of daily life.

How can we respond to the often repeated news of death? One clue lies in the fact that the message of death always comes wrapped in fear. This dark death-notice reminds us that one day each of us also shall die! Such a dark message can be good and wholesome. The news that someone we know has died has the power to call forth from us a renewed dedication to living full and holy lives.

One response that we all can make—perhaps the first, the most important, and most sustained response—is prayer. This prayer can be the simple outpouring of energy from our hearts to those who have died and to their families. In this way, our prayer may respond even to the death of those we have never met. And even if very brief, this outpouring, provided it be sincere, can bring us—as well as the deceased and those directly affected by the death—into the divine flow of mercy and love. To remember with prayer those who have died is not only a holy and religious deed, it is also a sign of our faith in God's continuous care.

When death comes knocking at our door, touching our lives personally, it is always a sacred time and an occasion for the family to come together in prayer. The deaths of members of our family, of neighbors or members of our parish should call us as a family to lift them up to the heart of God. This, of course, can be done at the wakes or at the funeral services, but we should primarily pray for them within the home. In fact, before we obtain a floral wreath or take covered dishes of food to the home of the mourning family, we should remember the dead person and the family in prayer. The family meal is an ideal time for the entire family as a community to do this. When we have invited God into all those lives that a death affects, including our own, then this family prayer can flow on in many forms of compassionate care.

Besides these, there are other occasions that summon us, personally or as a family, to pray for our parents and grandparents, life partners, children or close friends who are no longer with us in body. Part of the fear of death is our fear of being forgotten. We fear that in death we will slip from the memory of those with whom we have shared life. Only a shallow and thankless people forget their holy dead. Only an ungrateful child can erase the memory of parents who gave the most magnificent of all possible gifts: life itself. The anniversary dates of the death of parents or others with whom we have shared our hearts are important feast days inviting us not to forget. These memorial days invite us to *remember* our holy dead: to bring back to life within our hearts all the fragments of life that we shared with them. Remembering includes prayer, for by that expression we are able to say what is beyond words. We can more concretely express our love for those who have died by making a pilgrimage to their graves. By this pilgrimage that flows from prayer, we honor our holy dead and rekindle the flame of memory and that of gratitude as well. When we are hindered from such a pilgrimage because of distance, we can visit the shrine of their burial in prayer. For those persons who understand the mystery of the Communion of Saints, distance and time are no barriers. Such times of prayer as these prepare us not only for the next time that the shadow of death will cross our home but also for our own deaths.

The Feast Day of the Holy Dead on November 2 and the Memorial Day observance in late spring are two special days that have been set apart for communal remembering of the dead. On these days, special prayers and pilgrimages as well as the celebration of Mass fittingly become part of our prayer life. Together with these communal days, each family has its own special feasts of the holy dead. If we are unable to remember the dates of the death of family members or friends, let us take time to look these dates up and record them on our family religious calendars. All these special days of remembering, when we can recall those whom we have loved and can by prayer be in communion with them, add a richness and depth to our personal and family prayer lives.

The most beautiful memorial we can give to those we love is not one made of stone but is a living memory that is nourished by prayer, gratitude and ever-deepening affection.

Come Death,
>   and be my counselor, my personal advisor,
>   as I meet the numerous challenges of my day.
The great and powerful are surrounded by their advisors
>   who assist them in making important decisions,
>   but I am a simple person without such wise
>   counselors.
Yet, I, even as a simple person,
>   must make choices and decisions
>   that will determine the course of my life
>   and affect the lives of others.
I, too, need guidance and wisdom.
So, come Death,
>   be near and shadow my day,
>   and pass your gray shadow
>   over the choices that I consider.

Remind me, friend and constant companion,
>   that life is indeed brief
>   and that today and its joys are fleeting
>   and may never come my way again.
Nudge me with your boney finger, Death,
>   and remind me that the only truly important things
>   in life
>   are my relationships:
>   with God, with those I love and with myself.
Show to me, dark friend of the underworld,
>   that balance sheet which proves
>   that those things we think important

are seldom truly of importance,
and those things we may think not important
are truly the telling things of our short, short lives.
Counsel me, teacher of the tombs,
in how time taken to drink in a sunset,
to marvel at the butterfly upon the leaf
or the faces of children at play—
how these times and others like them
are more valuable than gold or the most precious of
jewels.

Come angel of death,
and guide, this day, my choices in life.

Amen†

Blessed are You, Lord our God,
>who are the keeper of the Book of Life.
Today, I have learned of the death of <u>(name)</u>,
>and, as this type of news always does,
>it comes as a shock.
We know, Lord, that we all must die,
>and that You alone keep the dates of our death
>within Your Book of Life,
>but we still share the shock of death.
That news carries with it the shadow of fear,
>for it is a reminder that, someday, I too shall die.
Today, then, I pray for <u>(name)</u>
>who has passed through the doorway of death,
>and I pray for myself as well.

Lord, I am sorry that I missed opportunities
>to make life more enjoyable for <u>(name)</u>,
>sorry that I did not know him/her better than I did.
If in any way I may have failed him/her,
>I ask that You forgive me
>as I pray for his/her eternal peace.

I remember in my prayer
>the members of the family
>who surely are lost in sorrow at this time.

Support them with Your Holy Spirit
 and grant them the courage to embrace this tragic
 mystery
 as part of the plan of life.

Lord, may the news of this death
 be for me a holy message
 of how not to waste my todays,
 how not to be unprepared for the arrival of death
 in my own life.
May I best remember _(name)_
 by being grateful for life today
 and by loving You, my God,
 with all my heart, all my strength and all my mind.
Eternal rest to _(name)_,
 and divine consolation to all of the family.

Amen✝

PRAYER
ON THE ANNIVERSARY
OF THE DEATH
OF A LIFE PARTNER

Lord God, Lord of Life and Death,
>today, I recall the death of my beloved.

My heart still bears the stain of tears
>from that day of great loss.

Our lives had so become one
>that a part of me died
>when <u>(name)</u> died.

Like two rivers that had joined as one,
>our two lives flowed together
>in joyful communion and affection.

You, Lord and God,
>were the One who arranged our union,
>and You, Divine Mystery of Love,
>were the fire of love between us.

I recall today, in prayer,
>how he/she changed my life
>and called forth from me all that was good and holy.

Like a mirror, I saw myself reflected in him/her
>and so was able to face my failings and shortcomings
>in my struggle to be worthy of Your gift of love.

As I recall and relive that day of sorrow,
>I rejoice and am grateful
>for the great treasure of memories that I possess.

Those years together are alive
>and continue to nourish me with life.

I firmly believe that (_name_)
    has not ceased to exist but is alive,
    fully alive and happy within Your sacred embrace.
I firmly believe and know
    that love is beyond the touch of death
    and that our love for each other remains
    and awaits our final union together with You.

I seek, Lord, a favor from You:
    when the time comes for me to open the door of
        death
    and journey to You,
    grant that (_name_) may come and take my hand,
    guiding me along the dark and mysterious way
    which leads to the wedding feast of eternity.
Lord of Compassion,
    be with me as I await that day
    and grant eternal joy and peace to my beloved
    and to all the holy dead.

Amen†

Prayer on the Anniversary of the Death of a Parent

Lord, today is a day of memories for me,
  for on this day my father/mother died.
It was a day of great sorrow
  and of hope.
I still feel a sense of loss
  at the absence of my father/mother
  who gave to me the gift of life
  and who guided me along its early paths.
As I remember the events of that day,
  I am grateful to You, Lord of Gifts,
  for having given to me such a good parent.
I take delight in the memories
  of the good times that happened within our home
  as I recall the tears of that day of death.

My parents were my most important teachers
  and father's/mother's last lesson for me
  was about how to die at peace with You and with
    life.
May this prayerful remembrance of his/her death
  make me mindful of preparing today for my own
    death
  by living a good and holy life.
Today, on this anniversary of death,
  I celebrate the mystery of Your holy ones,
  among whom now lives eternally my father/mother.

As part of the web of life,
  I feel the presence of my father/mother now,
  here beside me,
  as I experience Your Divine Presence.

Gracious Lord, may he/she and all the holy dead
  live forever in the splendor
  of Your divine light and life.

Amen✝

Prayer
for a Parent Whose
Child Has Died

This may be a private reflection or a prayer shared by both parents.

Mysterious Lord of Life and Death,
    a very part of my own life has died
    in the death of my child.
My soul is weighed down with sorrow
    and bears the wound of a lifelong scar.
Send to me Your angel of consolation
    for the pain is heavy and deep.

Come to my aid, Lord of Mercy,
    for I lack the power of the holy parent, Abraham,
    who was willing, in obedience to Your command,
    to sacrifice to You his beloved son, Isaac.
Lord God, You who are also a parent
    surely know my pain at the loss
    of my beloved child, *(name)*,
    who has been taken from my side by death.
Do not take my tears and sorrow
    as a sign of my unbelief that all who have died
    are resurrected to eternal life in You,
    but, rather, see in these tears
    a sign of my great love for my child.
As I held her/him in the embrace of love,
    may You, her/his Divine Parent,
    hold her/him close to Your heart forever.

Help me, Lord,
>   for I do not seek to understand the why
>   of this mystery of death
>   as much as I desire to accept it in a holy way
>   and to be healed and once again whole.
Support me, my Lord and God,
>   and wrap me in Your gentle love
>   as I attempt to carry this bitter cross
>   as Your Son, Jesus, carried the cross
>   which You gave to Him.

Amen✝

PRAYER
ON THE ANNIVERSARY
OF THE DEATH OF A FRIEND

Lord of Life and Death,
    today, I remember the death of <u>(name)</u>
    whose life touched mine
    and added to the richness of my existence.
I pause to recall the good times that we shared together.

     pause for silent reflection

I am grateful that these are imperishable treasures
    which I will carry with me into eternity.
Within the mystery of Your divine plan,
    our life-pathways came together
    and blended as parallel pathways.
I am grateful today
    for all that we shared in our times together,
    for humor and work,
    for affection and trust,
    for the celebration of life.

Lord of Compassion,
    we are all sinners and in need of divine healing,
    so grant to <u>(name)</u> whatever is needed
    so that he/she can rejoice forever
    in Your divine friendship and eternal care.

Gracious Lord,
    I lift up into Your Divine Heart
    my friend
    and ask that You grant to him/her eternal peace
    and the perpetual company of Your saints.

Amen†

PRAYER FOR VISITING A GRAVE IN A CEMETERY

Appropriate occasions might be an anniversary of burial or death. Memorial Day or All Souls Day.

God of Abraham and of Moses,
    Lord of the Living, who visited Jesus within His
        grave
    and filled Him with the fullness of eternal life,
    hear our prayer this day
    as we come to the burial place of <u>(name)</u>.
With reverence, we visit this sacred shrine
    where his/her body was placed
    within the womb of the earth
    to await the final day of glory.
We pause in silence to be united with him/her.

    pause for silent prayer

Lord, we have come on this pilgrimage of prayer
    to keep the flame of love alive within our hearts.
As we read his/her name upon the marker-stone,
    we rejoice because that name has been written for
        all ages
    in the palm of Your divine hand.

May the breath of creation that surrounds this grave—
    in trees, grass and earth, birds and sun—
    join us in prayer.

May this pilgrimage remind us of what we already
   know:
   that nothing dies;
   rather, life is only transformed into new life.
Holy is this grave,
   holy this earth that has held in gentle embrace
   the bodies of all who are buried in this cemetery.

Lord,
   with reverence, we leave a wreath of worship at this
      grave,
   woven with love, adorned with memories
   and with our faith in the reality
   of that earthen Easter morning
   when all the holy dead shall rise
   in the splendor of Your glory.
Till that day, eternal rest to (*name*)
   and to all the holy dead.

   Amen†

Lord God,
    to those who have never had a pet,
    this prayer will sound strange,
    but to You, Lord of All Life and Creator of All
       Creatures,
    it will be understandable.
My heart is heavy
    as I face the loss in death of my beloved _(name)_
    who was so much a part of my life.

This pet made my life more enjoyable
    and gave me cause to laugh
    and to find joy in his/her company.
I remember the fidelity and loyalty of this pet
    and will miss his/her being with me.
From him/her I learned many lessons,
    such as the quality of naturalness
    and the unembarrassed request for affection.
In caring for his/her daily needs,
    I was taken up and out of my own self-needs
    and thus learned to service another.

May the death of this creature of Yours
    remind me that death comes to all of us,
    animal and human,
    and that it is the natural passage for all life.

May <u>(name)</u> sleep on
>in an eternal slumber in Your godly care
>as all creation awaits the fullness of liberation.

Amen✝

The Last
and
the
Beginning
Chapter

As we come to this the final chapter in our hand-book of worship for the home, we invite you to begin at the same time, the first chapter in your own blessing-prayer-worship book. Any blank book will do, whether leather bound or a spiral notebook. On those blank pages you are encouraged to compose your own prayers with which to celebrate the times that are special in your life. This book is meant to contain rituals that will help you to prayerfully remember personal and family feasts that are of unique importance to you. Another purpose is to provide space for you to copy down your favorite prayers, perhaps a long overlooked prayer from the family home of your child-hood. These ancient prayers can act as a compass, aiding you in your ongoing journey into the Mystery of God.

As you look at the clean white pages of your blessing-prayer-worship book, you may feel that you are incapable of writing prayers. The first thing to do is to put aside that log-ical fear and simply speak the longings of your heart. At the same time, the blessings, rituals and prayers in this book may give you an idea or even a pattern for your prayers. The beauty of any prayer lies in its relationship with truth and its foundation in faith. If your prayer or blessing is honest, then it will be beautiful. May this final—and at the same time beginning—chapter be the start of an adventure of personal worship for you and for your family. May it encourage you to continue to make your home—whether it be a simple room, an apartment, a bedroom shared with another aged person, a religious house, or a traditional family room—what the home has been throughout our rich heritage of worship: the basic parish church to which each home-dweller belongs. May this primal domestic church become the chapel from which you carry the gifts of prayer, worship and praise into the times when you gather with the larger Church. There, at your communal place of worship, the history of your personal and family prayer will give a new life and grace to the ancient and beautiful prayer of the Church.

There is no need to hurry to fill your book. When the time is ripe, it will be there awaiting the fruit of your life of prayers. May your prayerful use of this handbook allow the river of prayer to flow on and outward, healing all the cosmos and giving glory to God.

INDEX OF PRAYERS

EDWARD HAYS, a Catholic priest of the Archdiocese of Kansas City, is the co-founder and a moving spirit of Forest of Peace Publishing. He is the author of over thirty best-selling books on contemporary spirituality. He has also served as director of Shantivanam, a Midwest center for contemplative prayer, and as a chaplain of the state penitentiary in Lansing, Kansas. He has spent extended periods of pilgrimage in the Near East, the Holy Land, and India. He continues his ministry as a prolific writer and painter.